Signs

Signs

Michael W. Smith
with Wendy Lee Nentwig

TRANSIT®
a Division of Thomas Nelson, Inc.
www.ThomasNelson.com
www.transitbooks.com

Published in Nashville, Tennessee, by Tommy Nelson®, a Division of Thomas Nelson, Inc.

ISBN: 1-4003-0295-1

Printed in the United States of America
04 05 06 07 LBM 5 4 3 2

contents

introduction

Let me just start by admitting that I don't have all the answers. I haven't found the secret to living the perfect Christian life or how to avoid pain and hurt. If that's what you're looking for, you can stop reading right now. Now that we have that cleared up, I can tell you I do have some stuff figured out. After years of living the Christian life, I've learned a thing or two, and I'm more than happy to pass it on. So expect some direction and advice that might just help you in your walk. You'll even find a few answers contained within these pages, but understand there's also a lot of mystery when it comes to God and the Christian life.

Those unknowns can really get to you if you let them. A "why?" here and a "how come?" there can start to add up until you begin to wonder what you know for sure anymore. I'm here to assure you there's plenty we can and do know. God is at work all around us and there are signs of His love and care for us everywhere. All you need to do is open your eyes.

That's what this book is meant to be. Consider it an eye exam of sorts. A pair of spiritual glasses to help you see more clearly what God wants you to be about as you move through this world. And I'm sharing it with you now because you're at an important place in your life. You face decisions that will shape who you become and what your life will be about. When I was growing up, there were people who did the same for me so I'm merely returning a favor. They were key people who had a huge impact on my life. Guys like the youth leader in the little town in West Virginia where I grew up who helped steer me in the right direction. They answered my questions and helped me make sense of what we can't know for sure this side of Heaven.

As the next generation, you're our future. You have the power to do amazing things for God and I want to help equip you to fulfill that promise. In fact, in the Old Testament book of Jeremiah God makes it clear He has big plans for you: "'For I know the plans I have for you,' declares the Lord. 'Plans to prosper you and not to harm you, plans to give you hope and a future'" (Jeremiah 29:11).

You'll find that's a theme throughout this book: Follow the signs to what God has for you. You may already have an idea or it may be a complete surprise. Either way, figure out what that plan is, what you're meant to do in this life, and you've won 90 percent of the battle. It will set things in motion. There's a great big world out there and God has plans for the part you'll play in it. So open your eyes and get ready!

"FOR I know the plans I have for you," declares the LORD, "plans to prosper you and not to harm you, plans to give you hope and a future."

—JEREMIAH 29:11

chapter one

signs

There are signs everywhere—literally. Drive down the highway, and you'll see billboards advertising everything from shopping malls to TV shows to 99¢ hamburgers. Some modern churches even rely on that kind of "roadside reading" to invite people to their weekly services. And most people don't think a visit to New York City is complete without a stop in Times Square to see the oversized signs featuring the models-of-the-moment showcasing the latest from Calvin Klein, Tommy Hilfiger, or Gap. Follow that up with a quick glance up or down the street, and you'll see theater marquees advertising the various Broadway shows being performed inside. Even if you live in a small town like the one I grew up in, you can't escape signs. Fast-food spots, grocery stores, and gas stations all use them to catch our eye.

While it's true that God hasn't resorted to renting out billboards to get our attention (although a Texas-based company did that on His behalf a few years back, featuring provocative messages signed by "God" in an attempt to turn drivers' thoughts to spiritual matters), He does use signs to communicate with us just the same.

God may choose to forgo neon and flashing lights, but all you have to do is look around to find countless signs that He exists. There are reminders everywhere. Whether I'm hiking at my farm in Franklin, Tennessee, or driving through my neighborhood, if I just open my eyes, I can't help but be reminded that God is close by.

Maybe I see the signs because I'm a big nature guy anyway. I'm all about taking time to stop and smell the roses, or, in the case of one memorable afternoon, the Bradford pear trees. It may sound silly, but about six years ago I was driving through my adopted hometown of Franklin, Tennessee, and the Bradford pear trees were in full bloom. Before I even had time to think about it, I had pulled off to the side of the road to get a closer look. I know it's weird, but suddenly tears began to well up, and I sat there and cried. I don't know if it was just one of those "God moments," but looking up and seeing God's creation there in full bloom overwhelmed me. It was an amazing reminder of the One who made us all. And why not expect amazing reminders from an amazing God?

Now, I'm not suggesting you seek out the nearest tree and try to drum up a few tears. (I can hear you breathing a huge sigh of relief at that news.) It's just that sometimes when we're looking for God, we're waiting for the big lightning bolt, while there are *little* reminders all around us. In other words, the big thing is: don't miss the little things. They're everywhere. All you have to do is walk outside.

YIELD

Why not take a walk somewhere off the beaten path today? Take time to really notice God's creation. If He put that much care into crafting a single leaf or beetle or feather, just imagine how much more care He put into you!

MISSING THE SIGNS

God doesn't just use signs to remind us of His presence. I believe He also uses them to help point the way. But in order to tune into this type of direction, you need to be on the lookout.

Have you ever been in the car when the driver missed a sign for the exit or street that he needed and you ended up lost or had to backtrack to reach your destination? Maybe he was too distracted to notice the sign that would have pointed the car in the right direction. He wouldn't be alone. One of the biggest problems we all face in America today is that we're surrounded by distractions, and we live way too fast. We find ourselves running from school and work to activities that range from baseball practice to hitting the mall to play rehearsals. Calling it "multi-tasking" may make it sound like we have it under control, but it doesn't change the fact that many of us are so caught up in our everyday lives that we're just too busy to see what's right in front of us. And that's when we miss the signs.

If I had my way, I'd install one of those big, yellow SLOW signs on every corner. Okay, that might seem extreme, but I really believe that God is telling us to *slow down*. Not that I always listen. I'm the first to admit, there have been periods when I've become completely caught up in being busy. Great opportunities came my way, and there were times I probably said yes when I should have said no. Sound familiar? It's a tempting trap to fall into, but in the end, it can leave little time for God and the business He really wants us to be about.

I learned that particular lesson the hard way. Fortunately, I *did* learn it, though. I found that the older I got, the easier it was to pass on the stuff I don't necessarily feel called to do. I know what you're thinking, but this isn't one of those "do as I say, not as I do" moments. I just know that if you can learn that lesson earlier than I did, you'll be ahead of the game and save yourself some heartache.

Of course, to know what to say no to, you'll have to determine what to say yes to. In other words, what are you called to? I can't figure that out for you, but I can tell you that if you don't slow down, you'll almost certainly miss it. It's like those road signs I was talking about. God offers direction, but if you're flying by at 80 miles an hour, chances are you won't have time to see it.

And don't expect Him to hit the brakes for you. It has to be your choice to slow down and read the signs. Sometimes they'll come in the form of advice from someone older and wiser. Parents, youth leaders, and spiritually mature friends can all be used by God to point you in the direction you should be going. What you enjoy doing and feel passionate about also factors in.

YIELD

Take a minute to take stock of your natural gifts and abilities. What do you enjoy doing? What do others say you do well? What do you get the most enthusiastic about? These questions can provide clues to your calling.

A lot of times, I think God speaks through the voices of others. I honestly believe that having people I trust and allow to offer input into my life makes all the difference. There's a faraway friend who challenges me and leaves me such encouraging phone messages that they could literally sustain me for a year. Then there's my pastor, Don Finto. We meet up for long walks in the woods, during which he continues to mentor me and spur me on. I don't think there's anything greater than having people who are willing to speak into my life, helping to shape me into the person God wants me to be.

For me, the formula is easy: I surround myself with people who have a lot of wisdom, and then I make a point to listen to what they say. Who do you have in your life that challenges you and holds you accountable? It may not be a pastor or a friend who lives a few states away. Family can fill that role as well. Now, don't roll your eyes at the thought that Mom or Dad might be able to provide some insight. Even more incomprehensible, what about one of your brothers or sisters? Someone doesn't have to be old to be wise. I know that I'm constantly learning things from my kids. It can be little things, maybe something one of them says out of the blue, and I will know it was from the Lord. It comes back to being open, to opening your eyes and looking around so you can see the signs.

Even with all that input, I still haven't "arrived." Finding out where you're meant to be is a continual process. After more than two decades of making music and ministering to others, my biggest challenge right now is still figuring out what it is I'm really supposed to be involved in. All these years later, I'm still asking the question because I find from year to year—or even from month to month or day to day—the answer changes. I need to continually check in with God to see what He wants me to be involved in today.

Once I do that, though, the work is just beginning. As a result of discovering what to say yes to, there is a lot of stuff I've got to say no to as well. If you're like me, that can be hard to do because I love to help out whenever I can. But I finally had to learn that emotionally and physically I just can't do it all. When you try to do everything, you end up doing nothing well. As a result, you're not able to excel at the stuff you're really called to do. When that happens, everyone loses.

Caution: Detour Ahead

Once you're on the right path, you still can't expect the ride to always be a smooth one. You can take your eyes off the road for just a minute and find yourself off track. Or maybe a pothole in the road or some unexpected engine trouble has you rethinking the journey you're on. "Surely, it would be easier to turn back or take a safer, more comfortable route," you hear yourself saying.

It's just that easy for doubt to creep in. We all experience those moments. No matter how strong your faith is, certain situations can cause you to wonder, *God, where are You?* We know that He's promised to never leave or forsake us, but when life doesn't turn out quite like we expect, it can be easy to feel as if we're suddenly all alone.

Fortunately, He's never really far away. When you find it hard to "feel" God, once again, all you have to do is open your eyes and you can see evidence that He's right here with us. I believe this so strongly that I even wrote a song about it. I was at George Lucas's Skywalker Ranch doing some recording (talk about inspirational!) when the idea came to me. I kept thinking, *Maybe this song is just supposed to get people to open their eyes, to see that all along the journey there are signs pointing the way.* That was it. I didn't have the lyrics, but I knew it would be called "Signs." I was in such a creative mode while at the ranch that I was continuously writing new music in between cutting finished songs. It was right there in the middle of the control room that I put together the tune for "Signs," writing the music on the spot, using a borrowed melody from one of my earlier, unfinished pieces.

It wasn't a brand-new idea. For years we've been singing, "Open the eyes of my heart, Lord," thanks to another songwriter, Paul Baloche. And other equally inspirational tunes find us asking God to show us what He wants us to see. But I couldn't help but think, *If I need another reminder, other people probably do, too.*

Despite the initial inspiration, it was a hard song to write. At first, we thought about cleverly tying together phrases from past songs, but we eventually scrapped that. Ideas from other collaborators were set aside as well because they just didn't seem right. In the end, the words came from my oldest son, twenty-year-old Ryan, who was inspired by John Bunyan's classic book, *Pilgrim's Progress*.

When he came to me and said, "I think I've got it," I could see the gleam in his eye, and I knew he was right. I'd read the book a long time ago, but Ryan is an avid reader and a real thinker, with an amazing book collection. I don't know why he went to *Pilgrim's Progress*, but I'm glad he did.

It's only fitting that I would write a song that would encourage others who might be feeling discouraged as they travel this road of faith. On the road, I'm constantly hearing reports from people of the amazing and wondrous things God is doing in their lives. Once again, I'm reminded that there are signs all around us.

That may lead you to ask another question: why does God continue to send us fresh signs of His love and care for us when He's already done more than we can ask or imagine, when He's already sent the ultimate sign of His love, His Son, Jesus? I think the answer is pretty simple: it's because He knows we need them. Life is hard

YIELD

Who can help you see the signs when your vision gets cloudy? What circumstances has God used to remind you of His love?

enough as it is, so He sends us little reminders that He's still here. I already know that to be true, but it's still something that I can't hear (or see) enough.

under construction

When you're young, it's easy to feel somewhat indestructible. I know there were times when I was a little reckless (often out of good intentions). Sometimes good things can come from zeal. That "I'm gonna live forever!" feeling can make it possible to be bold for God. Just remember: wherever you are in the process, you're still under construction. Your spiritual life will always be a work in progress.

These days, I'm more careful, more cautious. I'm not so busy running ahead because I'm more mindful of not wanting to miss anything along the way. Even so, I'm just as enthusiastic about trying to pinpoint my current calling. For me, it could be just a feeling I have as I really get down to the core of what I'm called to do. Lately, I start by asking myself the question, "How am I supposed to spend the rest of my days?" It's as simple as that. From there, I continually pray that God will make it very clear to me.

So what is He showing me? Right now, I think I'm called to write songs that reflect the heart of God. That's my goal, and hopefully it's a godly goal, because I believe I've yet to create my best work. In praying and listening to God, I believe He'd have me write something musically that's so compelling that everyone, across all lines, is drawn in.

It's scary and it's exciting. In the meantime, I know I'd better be getting ready so God can work through me. I'm the conduit. Like a cable modem, I'm not creating the messages and pictures that you'll see on your computer or TV screen; I'm just carrying the signal.

There have been times in the past when I wasn't ready. For years, there was talk of me recording a worship project. There were all kinds of signs that I was supposed to do it, but I fought against the idea. I was fearful for the wrong reasons, worried about what people would think, afraid they would say I was jumping on a bandwagon or seeking some new type of success. In the end, I did the record, and *Worship,* as it came to be called, was embraced by millions of people around the globe. It opened up a whole new area of ministry for me and changed my life and my career. A second album, *Worship Again,* followed, receiving a similarly warm reception and causing huge crowds and single worshipers to open their hearts and raise their voices to Him.

And all I had to do was follow the signs so God could work through me. What does God want to accomplish through you today?

What is God asking of you today? If you're still unsure, follow the signs. Is God using circumstances or people in your life to point the way? If you still feel like your future's a mystery, ask those you trust for some spiritual counsel. Chances are, they'll have an easier time seeing in you the godly potential you are overlooking. From then on, there will be no stopping you!

What is your real job? Is God nudging you in a particular direction? Look around. Follow the signs!

look for the signs

open
your
mind

chapter two

freedom

Freedom. It's a word that's used often in our post-9/11 world. As a country, we celebrate it, we fight to preserve it, we debate what it really means. In our personal lives, freedom is something we're usually clamoring to get more of. As a teenager, that may mean trying to negotiate a later curfew, a car of your own, or doing more with your friends without supervision. But freedom's about more than just politics or permission to come home after eleven.

For some, freedom is a dream that seems just out of reach. Turn on the news or pick up a newspaper, and it's not hard to find stories about people who are *literally* dying to come to the United States. Refugees risk their lives and the lives of their family members by traveling illegally in the back of a semi-truck with little air, water, or food or by attempting to sneak across our southern border under the eye of watchful guards. Some resourceful but misguided Cubans even tried to land on our shores in an old car they turned into a raft.

While America certainly has its problems, we do enjoy a level of freedom here that is practically unheard of in many other parts of the world. Just walk up and down the aisles of your local grocery store or glance at the directory at your local mall to see how many options we have available to us. Everywhere you turn, there are choices laid out before you. Pick a movie you want to see, and you can often choose between several theaters where it's playing, or you can at least select a time that fits your schedule. Once inside, you can choose to get popcorn, candy, or both (assuming your allowance is big enough). And it doesn't end there. You can sit up close; you can sit in the back row; you can talk during the previews; you can leave before the movie's over. And that's just one small area of life. Choosing a college major, extracurricular activities, a boyfriend or girlfriend, even the drive-thru window presents you with a mountain of choices.

Some of these decisions are made with careful consideration, while others you probably take for granted. We're faced with so many possibilities that it's easy to forget just how fortunate we are.

No matter what country you call home, though, no matter who's in power or what laws are passed or family rules are made to limit what you can say, wear, or do, there is one freedom we all share: we're all free in Christ. I know that sounds like something you've heard your pastor say a million times, but have you ever thought about what it really means? From the minute we enter this world, circumstances we have no control over can make life unfair. Why were you born in America while another child began life in a war-torn, drought-stricken nation in Africa? Why does your family struggle to make ends meet while your friends get to go on expensive vacations every summer? Why did you inherit Uncle Earl's big ears and your dad's unmanageable curls, while your sister has silky-straight hair and an adorably tiny nose?

The bad news is, there's nothing you can do about your ears, short of plastic surgery (which I don't recommend!). The good news is, God has forever settled the score. He's balanced the scales by sending His Son to die for us. When it comes to life in Christ, we're all starting at the exact same point. We're all of equal value to Him, and we're all equally free.

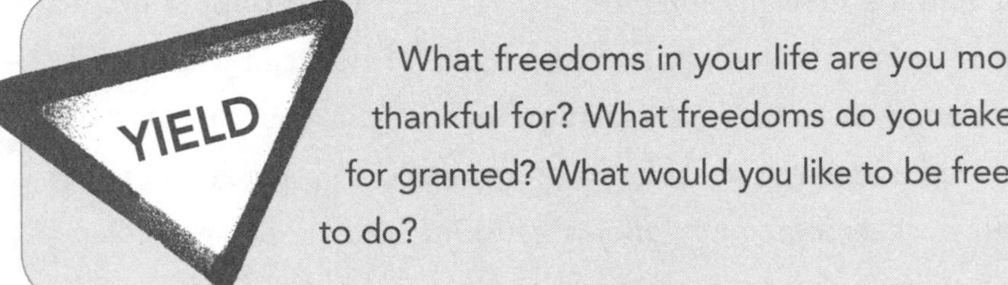

What freedoms in your life are you most thankful for? What freedoms do you take for granted? What would you like to be free to do?

THERE'S ALWAYS A CATCH

It's been said that with freedom comes responsibility. Or, as the Bible puts it, "From everyone who has been given much, much will be demanded" (Luke 12:48). In other words, freedom didn't come without a cost. While God doesn't have a "use it or lose it" policy, you are responsible for making the most of what you've been given. Does that sound a little overwhelming? It might if what you've done so far with the freedom you've been given is to master every video game available or put that sharp mind to use by memorizing large chunks of dialogue from the Lord of the Rings trilogy so you can quote it to your friends. Not that I'm saying you need to throw away your video games or stop seeing movies—God wants us to have fun in a wholesome way—I'm just reminding you that there is also work to be done.

You (and only you) are responsible for making good on the gifts God's given you. We've already established that in America you are fortunate enough to have the opportunity to pursue almost anything. When thinking about what you might accomplish, the possibilities are almost endless. So where do you start? At the beginning.

We talked in the last chapter about identifying your gifts. Once you've done that, it's time to try on some different opportunities and see what fits. Are you a computer whiz? How can you use that knowledge to further God's kingdom? Maybe you can start by building a Web site for your youth group to help reach other students or teaching computer classes to inner city kids and looking for opportunities to share your faith as you share your skills. Mission trips are also a great way to put your talents to good use while giving back a small part of what you've been given. From teaching Vacation Bible School, participating in drama ministry, or getting your hands dirty by repairing churches or schools in poor neighborhoods around the corner or across an ocean, there are tons of ways to try out work that piques your interest.

Now, I'll warn you, it can be a little scary at first to get out of your comfort zone. Doing something new while you're far from home or in an unfamiliar setting can throw you a bit. But it's at those times when we're weak that God is waiting there to help prop us up—so lean on Him. And after all, what's a little initial discomfort if you can use the freedom and gifts you have to change someone's life?

YIELD

Are there opportunities right in front of you that you've been overlooking? Has God been nudging you toward something that you've been afraid to try? What small step can you make today toward taking that on?

TOO MUCH OF A GOOD THING

When you were little, did your parents keep your holiday candy out of reach or limit the amount of cookies and soda you could consume? Do they still limit the number of activities or nights out with friends you're allowed in a given week, month, or school year? While these limits can be frustrating at times, they're there because your parents already know what you're still learning: too much of a good thing can become a bad thing. Whether it's eating an entire package of cookies and feeling sick afterward or joining every club and juggling several sports along with advanced placement courses until you wind up with mono or strep throat, if you don't manage your freedom, you can start to feel more like a prisoner than someone who's really free.

The Apostle Paul understood this way back in New Testament

times when he wrote, "'Everything is permissible for me'—but not everything is beneficial" (1 Corinthians 6:12). Just because we *can* do something, it doesn't mean we *should*. Some people take freedom too far. That's why in America, we have laws to protect us from ourselves and each other, and at home we have rules to do the same. Sometimes it seems like the more freedom we have, the more rules we need. While I love having so many options, I can't help wondering if some of the people I've met in much poorer countries, people we would quickly label "less fortunate," aren't more free in the ways that really count.

In America, there's always something newer and better to chase after. College kids are handed credit cards and allowed to buy expensive items they don't have the money to pay for. We're told daily that we "deserve" a new car, designer clothes, the latest gadget. This "gimme more" lifestyle can leave you feeling anything but free. I'm not immune to that either. But what I've discovered as I've chased after things and watched my friends do the same, is that freedom really comes when you stop chasing and find happiness right where you are.

FREE AT LAST

For me, creative freedom came in the form of an instrumental project titled *Freedom*. It let me express myself musically in ways I hadn't on previous CDs, and I was able to combine my love of movie scores and symphony sounds with songs that didn't have to conform to the rigidity of the usual verse-chorus-verse-chorus way of songwriting. Not that I don't love singing a great pop song or leading crowds of Christians in a powerful worship tune, but this type of music is a gift I feel called to cultivate.

It wasn't what most people expected from me. I was extremely grateful for the success I had experienced making Christian pop, and I was sensitive to the fact that many people were hoping I would deliver more of the same. But with God's guidance, I knew what was right for me, and that gave me the courage to take the more unpredictable path.

It's something I've been doing much of my life. College would have been a safer bet (and probably would have had my parents breathing a sigh of relief), but with some divine direction, I set out to chart my own unique course. I arrived in Nashville with my musical talent and little else. There were tough times, and it's not a road I'd recommend for everyone, but it was right for me at the time. And as my career took off and there was the temptation to become more structured and think ahead three, five, or even ten years, I chose not to do that. While there may be times when I could have planned more or been a little more disciplined, I believe it's important to never have my life so planned out that I lose the freedom to follow wherever God might lead me next.

Fortunately for me, my number one goal has never been to come up with a ten-year plan. I don't think I'd even know how to go about it. It's not part of how I'm wired. Anyway, I don't want to get too distracted with that because I know that it's what I do right now in the short-term, the decisions I make every day, that will shape what happens ten years from now anyway. So instead of trying to do any detailed, long-range planning, I just continue to ask God, "What's next?"

Of course, that doesn't mean I don't have dreams I'd like to see become reality. I'd love to score another film. I'd love to go out and do symphony shows and to travel to Africa, and I'm willing to make the necessary plans to make those things happen—if that's what God wants me to do. In the same way, you may want to become a marine biologist or a fighter pilot, and both of those jobs will require some planning. You can't sit back and wait for someone to hand you a lab coat or a flight suit and welcome you to the team. There's a procedure to follow. So understand, I'm not advocating having no plan, I'm saying don't have your life so rigidly planned that there's no room for God to move.

Some might call it living on the edge, but I see it as staying open to whatever God wants to do. And it's when I'm there, in that place, that I feel like I have the greatest potential to do my best work. That attitude has led to some of my best songs. It also impacts my live shows. Just last night, I called my keyboard player and said, "I've got a different way I want to open the show tonight." As a result, we are all scrambling, but I love it because the show's going to feel completely different and be exactly what God wants it to be.

There are others who have taken being open to God to even greater extremes. While revered later in her life for her work with the poorest of the poor in India's slums, Mother Teresa wasn't always applauded for stepping outside the lines. Initially, she had to fight her superiors for permission to live out her calling the way she knew God wanted her to. And even once she was allowed to follow the path set before her, it wasn't an easy one. She was surrounded daily by people who were suffering before dying horrible deaths. It wasn't an easy road or a call most of us would find easy to follow.

Another person closer to home who challenged me was fellow musician Rich Mullins. Before he died in 1997, we were still becoming friends. While we didn't spend a lot of time together because he was rarely home, his lifestyle intrigued me. He could pack everything he owned into a space the size of half my office. Because of his choice to not let material possessions tie him down, he could live in a tent or on an Indian reservation. I think I envied that a little bit. While his music was successful and he touched hundreds of thousands of people with his songs, he took a minimal annual salary and gave away much of what remained.

I remember asking myself at one time, "Why am I not doing that?" and "Should I be doing that?" But that was Rich's path, not mine. I have a family, and while I respect it, I'm not called to that particular lifestyle. Still, there was something about it that was very challenging. So while I don't live that way, I know I'm not afraid to live that way. I think I could do it. And that's the key: while I may not be called to walk away, it is important to know I could. We each need to learn to hold things loosely, to know that there is nothing in this life that you couldn't give up if He asked. That's when you know you're really free.

My life has been shaped by turning right when everyone else was going left. If I hadn't been open to taking the untraditional route, I wouldn't be where I am today. But there will always be pressure to do the obvious thing. After all, the road less traveled is called that for a reason. If you venture off the familiar path, you might feel lonely at times. You might have moments of wondering what on earth you're doing. There may even be days when you find yourself asking God, "I thought this was where You wanted me. Why isn't it working out?" Despite that occasional uncertainty, I can tell you without a doubt that there's no better, safer place to be than in the center of God's will.

what plans have you made for your life? Are they your plans or God's? Will you take an untraditional or a more conventional route to get there? What do you think God might want to teach you along the way?

look for the signs

chapter three

Missing Person

I was on a plane with my longtime collaborator and friend, Wayne Kirkpatrick, when it happened. It all started when I played him a new song, "Missing Person," which I was planning to include on an upcoming album. It was more than just a musical moment. Soon enough, the message behind the tune had us both feeling convicted. As we zoomed along, 30,000 feet up in the air, talking about the intense passion we used to have for God, I couldn't help but get a little depressed. What happened to that fire that I had been so sure was unquenchable? Before long, though, I was past feeling depressed and had moved on to feeling determined. I wanted to get that fire back.

Throughout my career, God has used me to sing songs that have helped fan those flames in young hearts and rekindle a spiritual passion in Christians who find their faith stuck in neutral. But those messages aren't just for music fans, they're for me as well. And this one was coming through loud and clear. It wasn't as if I had turned my back on God or anything like that. In fact, if you ran into me on the street or attended one of my concerts, you probably wouldn't have a clue. But it's hard to be a Christian for years and never find that early enthusiasm dimming just a bit. I wasn't the only one to experience it, either. The message of the song hit home with Wayne and many of the other people I played it for as well. It seemed like it was a pretty common problem.

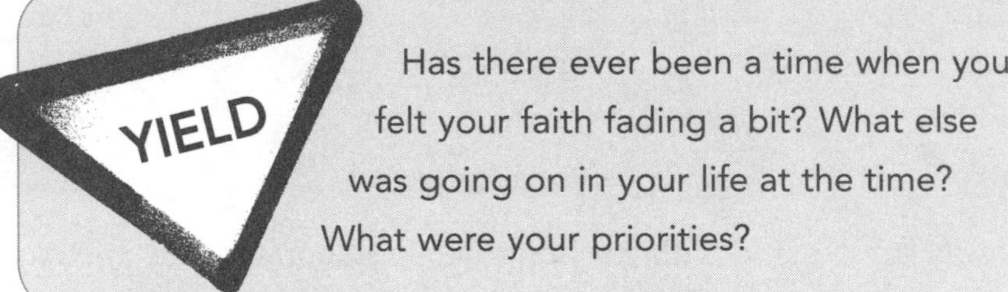

Has there ever been a time when you felt your faith fading a bit? What else was going on in your life at the time? What were your priorities?

complex problem, simple solution

Fortunately, there's a pretty simple solution. There are steps we can take to get that fire of faith burning bright again in our lives. In fact, there are a lot of ways to turn around that all-important relationship with Jesus, but it usually starts with simply abiding in Him, in other words, following where He leads.

Sounds easy enough, but it's where a lot of us get off track. As we cruise along in our daily lives, regular demands begin to crowd in and take up time that should be God's. Between school, friends, church, sports, family, hobbies, TV, and video games, it's easy to have little left over. Soon enough, He's lost in the shuffle. That's why it's important to make a point to set aside time to spend with God. You might feel silly penciling the Creator of the universe into your calendar, but you do no less for other important activities, don't you?

What do I mean? Well, if you're on the soccer team at school, you have to show up for each practice and go through various drills and exercises to help you improve. You can't just talk about playing soccer and put pictures on your wall of world-class players and expect to get better. It's only through regular interaction and effort that you grow as a team and develop the necessary skills.

In the same way, you can't just wear a Christian T-shirt or put a fish sticker on your locker and think that alone will bring you closer to God. That's all outward stuff (and it's fine with me), but God wants to be a part of what's going on inside, too—in your heart. The

YIELD

How do you currently go about connecting with God? Do you set aside time regularly to spend with Him—reading, praying, or worshiping on your own? If not, how can you begin to incorporate that into your daily schedule? Who can you find to hold you accountable to doing that or help you in learning how to make it part of your everyday life?

other important relationships in your life all require time and attention, and, in that way, this relationship is no different.

So once you've made time in your schedule, where do you go from there? With friends, you can talk on the phone, hang out, even go see a movie, but you can't very well take God to the local multiplex. That doesn't mean you can't spend time with Him in different ways. Reading the Bible and praying are great opportunities to connect with God. Sure, they seem obvious, but then how come they're so easy to overlook?

The Heart of Worship

One of the best places I've personally rediscovered that fire is in times of vertical worship. I almost hate to use the term *vertical worship* because it's been so overused, but it's become a personal crusade of mine to help people understand that worship is about much more than music. When I lead worship, I get a lot of compliments on the sound and on the songs, but that's just the beginning. Worship is a lifestyle. As for the word *vertical,* don't let that throw you either. It simply means up and down, or in this case, between God and you. It's not about who's in the pew next to you or what your best friend is doing or what happened in homeroom this morning. It's about you and God connecting. Sometimes it happens to me at the most unexpected times.

About three months ago at New River Fellowship, a young church plant I helped start, I walked in, and this guy was playing piano, and it was communion Sunday—and I just fell apart. All I could do was cry the whole service. I sat there on the front row and wept. I couldn't even pull it together to do the announcements, something I was scheduled to handle that morning. Instead, I got up, and I cried. One of our pastors, Rafael, had to come up and grab the announcements. I couldn't do it. And no, I wasn't having some sort of breakdown. I hadn't had a fight with my wife or lost my recording deal or found out a friend or family member was sick or hurt. It was just this brokenness of realizing all over again how much I need God. For some reason, on that particular morning, I tapped into that truth and found myself saying, "Hey, God, I'm desperate for You. I really am."

Now, just because I can point to spiritual moments in my life like that one, it doesn't mean I'm perfect, and I don't always live out that reality perfectly either. Sometimes I get distracted. But the important thing is that I realize that. I don't make excuses. I get back on track. And God looks beyond my good intentions and my mistakes. He looks inside and knows my heart, which can be reassuring because I strive to have a heart like King David. I may make mistakes, but deep down inside I really do desire to be a strong man of God. That's the good news. The bad news is, I don't always want to do the right thing. Sometimes the alternative seems much more appealing. But I know the consequences of sin. I know that I'm loved and that I have a purpose. I'm reminded of that during intimate encounters like the one I had at New River Fellowship or those I have with God any time of the day or night. And those moments change me and give me the courage and strength to do what I know is right.

If you spend time with God on a consistent basis, you'll find you start to change, too. As a result, you'll become less concerned about what you want to do and getting your own way. What you want will become closer to what God wants. Trust me, it's hard to get too off track when you're that in tune. And once you find that missing person inside of you, from there, you start looking outward. That's when I find myself asking, "How can I help someone? How can I pour my life into someone?" That's when you really start to become who God wants you to be: a servant.

That's where, in the last few years, I've found the greatest contentment. As I've tapped into taking care of others, the things I once thought were important have become much less so. Having a #1 song or a platinum CD or winning awards doesn't bring you peace. I won't lie and tell you it doesn't feel great, but it's nothing compared with being a part of changing someone's life. That's why what really gets me excited is when I visit Nashville's Rocketown club for teens and see kids who need to hear about God show up for concerts or coffee or to hang out in our skate park. It's the same emotion that wells up in me when I see another child sponsored through Compassion International, a Christian relief organization I've been involved with for years. Or sometimes it's as simple as pouring my life into a little kid at church who's not very well loved. Try it, and I guarantee that you'll start to experience some real joy in your life.

YIELD

What dreams or accomplishments are you chasing that you think will make your life complete? Are those aspirations in line with God's goals for you? Are you getting excited about the things that excite God?

Missing in Action

Unfortunately, some people never take the opportunity to turn things around. They think there will be time to get their spiritual life back on track later. Right now, they just want to have fun. There was a time in my life when I made my share of bad decisions and thought I'd have plenty of time later to put God first. In my mind, I still have painful memories of almost dying one night from a drug overdose; of playing an after-hours bar that I knew didn't fit with who God was calling me to be. These quick glimpses, like some sort of mental Polaroids, sometimes have me asking, "What if?" It's frightening to think what could have happened if I hadn't gone searching for that missing person that was me and found a gracious God waiting to welcome me back.

But how did a good, small-town, West Virginia boy get to that point in the first place? Pride may have been part of it. I thought I had it all figured out. This is something I'm much more watchful about now, and with good reason. In the music business, it can be hard to stay humble when there is no shortage of people waiting to tell you what you want to hear. It's a common practice at concerts for fans to line up afterward to shower the artist with praise, seeking autographs and sharing personal stories. While it's always nice to receive a compliment or know your hard work and talent is appreciated, if I don't watch it, I can start to believe the hype. That's why I need to have people who know me well and whose opinion I trust to keep me in check.

Selfishness can also play a role. Sometimes when you're young, you can be pretty self-centered, even out of good motives. You get out of high school, and you're consumed with trying to figure out what life is all about. It's all part of growing up, but you still need to be on the lookout. If I could go back and talk to my teenage self, I think I would tell him, "Don't forget the lonely; don't forget the poor; don't forget the less fortunate. They're all around you, but it's so easy to get so consumed with what you're doing that you don't even see them." I've always had a heart for reaching out to people, but in order to move from intentions to action everyone needs some direction and discipline, something you don't always make a point to seek out when you're young and anxious to try your wings.

Looking back on those days, I really wish I had more mentors in my life to guide me through that important time. I really could have used a group of men to mentor me during my younger years, people who would have held me accountable. I was a bit too much of a free bird. Like me, you may not think you need it right now, but I would encourage everyone to actively seek out this sort of relationship. Accountability isn't a luxury in the Christian life. Everyone needs to have spiritual mentors who can help guide you along the paths they've already walked and good friends who can help steer you back on course when you begin to veer off in the wrong direc-

YIELD

In what areas do you struggle most? Who can you get to hold you accountable in those areas? What measures can you take to help you avoid temptation in the future?

tion. It's also important to stay plugged in at church so the leaders there can hold you accountable. I didn't have enough of those relationships in the early days, and that's why, for four difficult and trying years, I was a mess. All because I didn't raise the standard, I didn't raise the bar, and I didn't surround myself with other godly men who would encourage me to do that. I thought I could do it on my own and that it would all be okay.

Even during that difficult time, though, there were still signs of God's love and care for me. The most important ones were my parents. Throughout my life, Mom and Dad have been two of my greatest examples. While I grew up in a Christian home, they didn't preach at me much. Sure, they got on me a little bit (they are parents, after all!), but mostly they taught by example. I watched my mom and dad love each other, and I watched how they treated everyone they came in contact with.

If you have a strong Christian family behind you, as I did, don't take it for granted. It's a gift not everyone has been given. If you don't have it, don't feel like that support is beyond your reach. Seek out strong Christians who can be good examples for you.

Preventative measures are great. Mentors, good friends who will hold you accountable, and a strong local church that you're involved in will go a long way toward keeping you on the right track. But it's also important to remember that if you do make a mistake, don't let it keep you from trying again. We serve a forgiving God who literally died to give you a second chance. All you have to do is ask. After all, we're all becomers. None of us has arrived.

There are choices I've made during the course of my life that I wish I could go back and change. Words I'd like to un-say. Mistakes I'd like to undo. But I also know that God has used those experiences to make me who I am today.

what regrets do you have today? what choices have you made that have pulled you away from god? what can you do to change that in the future? Are there areas of your life where you know you're in need of some accountability? what steps can you take today to make some changes?

open
your
mind

chapter four

friends

It's arguably my most popular song. Most nights, I can't get off the stage without singing it. It's also still a favorite on closing night at summer camps, and for years it's been a musical staple at graduation ceremonies across the country. That's pretty amazing considering it was really only meant to be heard by the members of a small Bible study group my wife and I took part in. One couple was moving on, and we wrote it to help send them on their way. Who could have imagined it would become a sort of anthem embraced by so many people?

I've been asked so many times, "Why do you think that song struck such a chord with so many people?" It obviously connected for some reason, and while I'd like to say it's the melody or my skillful piano playing, I think its popularity owes a lot to the subject matter itself.

Friendship is one of the most important things we have in this life. Don't believe me? Just try going through a really tough time without your friends to lean on, and you'll see what I mean.

YIELD

Who are the friends you would count on during a difficult time? What qualities do they have that make them such good friends? What makes you a good friend to others? Are there ways you can be a better friend to those around you?

While the song is a celebration of friendship, it's also bittersweet because it's about saying goodbye. Over the years, I've learned that the song has been extremely meaningful to people going through some kind of turmoil or strife, particularly the loss of a loved one. Maybe it's because when you go through a tragedy like that, you find out fast just how important friendship really is. While nothing can completely take away the pain, to look around and realize you have all these people loving you and supporting you can make all the difference in the world.

I've had so many people tell me about difficult situations that they have gone through, times that they believe they would never have survived if it hadn't been for their close friends who rallied around them. It's not surprising to find, then, that most of us value friendship more than any other thing in the world. I certainly know that I can't make it through this life without my comrades, the people who have seen me through the good times and the bad and stuck beside me no matter what.

I guess that's a really big part of why that song continues to live on. Although I'm sure there are some people who wish I would go ahead and retire it for good, I sang it the other night to a standing ovation. Even after all these years, it still has the power to bring a crowd of 10,000 people to their feet. It's incredible to see how God has used it to touch people's lives, and I'm grateful to be a part of that.

FOREVER FRIENDS?

Even if you've never sung "Friends" around the campfire, chances are you have peers in your life that you count on. Their names, faces, and level of importance may change through the years, but your need for that kind of connection in your life will never go away.

There have been times, I admit, when I was so busy, I felt like I hardly had time to have friends. There just wasn't much extra time to nurture friendships. At times I would feel a little left out, especially when I looked around and noticed that some people seemed to have these amazing best friends. These days, my best friend is my wife, Deb, but I know I still need to have other people in my life, guys I can talk to about anything. As my life and schedule have changed, I see God opening up the door for me to start to spend more time with some people I didn't think I'd ever have the opportunity to really get to know. That's exciting to me because I honestly think God has put each of them in my life for a reason.

You need friends in your life, too. It may not mean you'll have one best friend, though. Maybe you're one of those people who would rather have several close friends instead. The most important thing is that you find people you can connect with and be honest with, people who you allow to offer input and whose advice and opinions you respect.

Sometimes a close friendship develops with someone because you have so much in common. You like the same clothes, the same music, the same sports, the same TV shows. You're completely in sync, and that sure makes hanging out easy. At the same time, other friends may be a good fit because of how different you all are. It may be harder to agree on what movie to see on a Friday night with this group, but those relationships can be just as rewarding (and just as necessary). Both types of friends challenge you, but each in different ways.

One of the people who has been challenging me lately is my friend, Max Lucado. While I've known the popular Christian author and Texas-based pastor for a long time, our busy schedules—not to mention the fact that we live in totally different states—made it difficult to connect. Finally, we went on the road together when he joined Third Day and me for the Come Together and Worship Tour. That extended road trip gave us a chance to spend a ton of time together and become closer friends. It was great because once we got together, we remembered just how much we love each other and how much we enjoy being together.

In the beginning, I wasn't sure how much we would have in common, but Max has become an important friend in my life, and we connect in more ways than I originally thought. Even though the distance makes it difficult at times, I value all the good things he brings into my life. For starters, he's a real encourager. He believes in me and speaks life in me. That means a lot to me, and I hope I do the same for him.

As a result, we continue to make time to see each other, or at least talk on the phone, regularly. Sometimes, like last Saturday, that takes the form of a golf game in San Antonio, Texas. Other times it's a quick message on the phone. Whatever the means, we make it a point to connect.

Some friendships come about through a more interesting route. For instance, I love how being friends with somebody can lead to being friends with someone else. That's how I met Bono from the band U2. Since he makes his home in Ireland, Nashville isn't exactly next door, but he came through town in late 2002 to talk about an African Relief organization he helped found called DATA. I was at that meeting because I was interested in the cause, but I had no idea I'd come away with much more than some helpful information.

The charismatic musician-turned-activist was quickly becoming at home in the political arena in order to help raise funds for aid to African nations ravaged by AIDS, drought, and civil war. Through a strange series of events, I was already somewhat at home in that world, having established a friendship with the first President Bush and continuing to have a relationship with his son, George W. Bush, who now sits in the Oval Office. So because of my relationship with a president, I became friends with a rock star.

At first, I was simply asked to ride with Bono to his next stop. I quickly jumped in the van he was traveling in, and suddenly we were sitting right next to each other. In the beginning, it felt a little surreal, but soon enough we were deep in a conversation that lasted until we arrived downtown. At the time, I didn't expect anything beyond that. Still, I couldn't help feeling that God had somehow orchestrated our short time together.

Bono obviously knew I was friends with the president, and that was intriguing to him. I think he hoped that as a result of that relationship, I might be able to help him with his cause. While in Nashville, he was also stopping by the office of another friend of mine, Senator Bill Frist. So my connection to two politicians, unlikely friendships in their own right, led to my making another unique friend.

While Bono and I don't spend a lot of time together, we e-mail occasionally. We've also managed to connect in person at least a few times since that first meeting, including a stop at his house for lunch when I was visiting his home country. Our lives are quite different, but each sees something in the other that we admire. I enjoy his sense of humor and the way he encourages me, while I think he was touched by the close bond I share with my wife and kids.

That's how it is in true friendships—there's give and take. Even when one friend is the President of the United States and the leader of the free world. While you might wonder what I have to give in a relationship like that (trust me, I asked the same thing), I think we really do have a genuine friendship. Part of that is based on the fact that, unlike so many others in his life, he knows I don't want anything from him. That has to be a refreshing change for him. And it's a balance I'm careful to maintain. While I have my beliefs and my causes, I'm careful not to push them too hard when I visit Washington. The truth is, that's not why I'm in his life.

You may not have friends who regularly appear on the covers of magazines, but those relationships are just as important! And just like your relationship with God, these relationships need to be nurtured, too. Throughout your life, these are the people who are going to help shape you, who are going to challenge you, and who are going to provide insight when you need it most.

YIELD

On a scale of 1–10, how important are your friends to you? Are most of your friends a lot like you or are you and your best friend an unlikely pair? What can hanging out with someone different from you add to your life?

Just as friends can help steer you in the right direction, they can also lead you into all sorts of trouble. That's why it's important to pick your friends carefully. Having the wrong friends can be worse than having no friends at all. That latter option might seem lonelier, but you'll also be pretty lonely if you're spending months grounded, unable to leave the house.

In the same way, you can't always tell who you'll connect with based on your first impression or how much you have in common. Choosing friends from among your youth group or other kids who say they're Christians doesn't guarantee you'll be free of bad influences. Also, people can change, especially during the teen years when it's common to try on different styles and personalities to see which one fits. As a result, someone who was once closer than a brother can suddenly start doing things you'd never have dreamed possible.

So while I'm a huge advocate for friendship, you also need to take stock of those relationships every now and then. Ask yourself if the people you're spending the majority of your time with are building you up or tearing you down. Do they make it easier for you to walk with God or harder to follow Him? The answers to those questions should give you a pretty clear idea of when it's time to find a new crowd.

NO MAN IS AN ISLAND

Even Jesus needed friends while He was here on earth. John, Paul, and Luke—these men were His followers, but they were also His friends. Of course, Jesus could have gone it alone, but why would He? Why would you? Friends may not be a physical necessity like food or water, but they sure make life more bearable.

While who you eat lunch with in the cafeteria or hang out with on a Friday night may seem trivial in the grand scheme of things, God does care about who you call your friends. Just flip to your Bible's concordance and you'll probably find at least a dozen verses that talk about friends or friendship. From the friendship pacts between David and Jonathan or Ruth and Naomi in the Old Testament to the close bond of early missionaries Paul and Timothy in the New Testament, the Bible proves that God knows the value of a good friend. While times have certainly changed, I still think we can learn a lot from these old friends. Jonathan is a great example of selflessness while Ruth's devotion should be an inspiration to any friend. Meanwhile, Paul was not just a friend to Timothy, but also a mentor. And don't forget Mary and Elizabeth or Jesus and John the Baptist. They each offered comfort to the other during difficult times. So what does that mean for you? These relationships can be a great gauge for determining if our own friendships are based on godly principles. If they are, you have a friendship that is going to help you grow, instead of drag you down. And isn't that what true friendship should be about?

What does the word *friend* mean to you? Has reading this chapter changed how you view the impact (both good and bad) friends can have in your life? As you look back over your school years, who have been your closest friends? Do you still hang out, or have you drifted apart? For those friends you're currently close to, what connects you? What do you do when you spend time together? Are your close friends people who pull you closer to God or farther away?

Look for the signs

chapter five

This Is Your Time

Time. When you're young it's easy to believe there's an infinite supply of it, and instead of time marching on, as the saying goes, it seems to be dragging along. While waiting for summer vacation to finally arrive or enough months to tick by so that you're old enough to get your driver's license or go on a date, time can seem slower than ketchup coming out of an almost-empty bottle.

But eventually something happens that drives home the reality that life is short, and it's up to you to make the most of every moment. For me, one of those "somethings" that served as a tragic reminder was the 1999 shooting spree at Columbine High School in Littleton, Colorado. I knew life was precious long before I saw the horrible footage running in a seemingly never-ending cycle on CNN and virtually every other network. But after attending the memorial service, I couldn't get what had happened out of my mind. I was particularly moved by the story of one of the victims, Cassie Bernall, who reportedly stood up to the two classmates behind the shooting spree and declared her faith in God when asked if she believed, a decision that ended her life.

I found myself wondering how I would have responded if I were asked to lay down my life. Martyrdom isn't something we talk a lot about these days, especially in America. Of course, there are stories in the Bible, and we know that early Christians were at times put to death for their beliefs. We also occasionally hear stories coming out of current-day China, or other faraway places halfway around the world, about Christians meeting in secret home churches and being harassed or jailed for their faith. It's not something we imagine ever happening here, though, and so most of the time it's pretty easy not to think about. Sure, we might get teased for wearing a Christian T-shirt to the mall or harassed for bringing a Bible to school or choosing to maintain high moral standards when it comes to dating, movies, or bad language, but we don't fear losing our lives for what we believe.

After returning from Colorado, I remember trying to make myself imagine, "What if I had a gun pointed at my head and was asked if I believed in God? What would I say?" After a lot of soul-searching, I came to the conclusion that I think I would have responded with a "yes." I really do. And that realization was affirming once it sank in, believing I really would have done the same thing this brave teenager did. Of course, when you're suddenly put in that position, with no warning or time to prepare, and you know you could lose your life in a matter of seconds all depending on what you do, none of us can say for sure how we'd react. It's a pretty unbelievable place to be in. But we can at least hope that we would do the right thing.

YIELD

Do you think you would be strong enough to admit your belief in God if your life depended on it? Why or why not? Have you ever had to stand up for your faith in smaller ways, at school or with friends, and faced ridicule because of it? How did you respond?

From that, a new song was born, inspired by Cassie's bravery and my own reaction to the tragedy. Because of its emotional roots and the amazing story behind it, "This Is Your Time" will always be a celebration of Cassie's life and faith. More than four years later, the song is just as relevant, and while I know people still think about Cassie and remember that it was inspired by the events at Columbine, it's also become a great way to evangelize—to believers and nonbelievers alike. It's also become a charge for those of us still here to make the most of the hours, days, months, or years we have left because we never know when our time on this earth may run out. The truth is, it's a message we all need to hear from time to time.

YIELD

If your life ended tomorrow, what regrets would you have? What would you wish you had done that you never had the courage to do? What small ways could you have made more out of the time you had? What can you do differently starting right now to make sure you're getting the most out of every moment?

WHEN GIVING UP IS GOOD

For some of us, we can't say yes to the question, "Would you die for Him?" because we've never really answered the question, "Will you live for Him?" You may be going through the motions, attending church, youth group, and summer camp, and you may even know how to talk the talk. You're fluent in Christianese, have the requisite fish symbol on your car, and carry your Bible around in a big, padded cover complete with a pocket for multicolored highlighter pens to turn God's Word into a neon rainbow of pertinent passages.

Despite what it looks like from the outside, there's something wrong on the inside. You've never really surrendered your life to Him. You're still convinced that you can do it on your own, not willing to submit to the surprise twists and turns a life led by God is sure to contain. Or maybe you have surrendered to Him—mostly. There are still a few areas you'd rather keep for yourself. I mean, you have such a vested interest in them, after all, and you just want to make sure things go as planned where this stuff is concerned.

Following God doesn't really have to be an all-or-nothing

proposition, does it? you wonder. According to the Bible, it does. In Revelation 3:16 Jesus says, "So, because you are lukewarm—neither hot nor cold—I am about to spit you out of my mouth." If you haven't gotten the message yet, God wants your whole heart.

YIELD

What areas of your life are you keeping for yourself, unwilling to surrender them to God? What are you afraid will happen if you follow God's plan for these areas instead of your own? Will you have to let go of things you enjoy? Will you miss out on something you really want? How can you work toward giving those up and trusting God to change your desires?

Finders, Keepers

For some, I think "This Is Your Time" finds them considering the gospel message and saying, "I've never really believed it before, but maybe this thing is true." It's become a song for seekers, and I find myself dedicating it to them often. Several years after the song was written, I still have people coming up to me and reporting that they became a Christian as a result of that song, which is an amazing thing to hear. They came to a concert or began listening to one of my CDs as a seeker and then they became a finder. What could be better than that?

For those of us who have already accepted Christ, whether

months or years ago, it's not just a call to make the most of our lives, but I also see it as providing a sort of spiritual checkup to make sure we're keeping God first. To me, it says, "This is your moment, right now, to consider where you stand with the Lord." I believe that due to the background of the song, it makes nearly everyone who hears it automatically reexamine where they are on this all-important issue in life: your relationship with God. Are you right with God? Are you not right with God? These are questions we should all be asking ourselves regularly. You never know when your life will end, and it will be too late to do anything about it.

That wasn't the only thinking Columbine had me doing, though. My time spent in Colorado was also life changing because I came back and honestly began to question, "Am I really doing what I'm supposed to be doing? Am I seizing every opportunity? Am I really living life or am I just serving myself? Am I doing

YIELD

Which question most applies to you? Are you a seeker considering whether the Bible is true? Are you a Christian who needs to reconsider whether you're putting God first? Are you a committed believer who needs to take this opportunity to ask God if you're doing what He really wants, seizing every opportunity and making the most of life for yourself and those around you?

enough for others?" Those are hard questions to ask, especially when you know the answers will likely require action on your part. But I did answer those questions, and then I rolled up my sleeves and got to work.

One of the biggest results of that line of questioning for me was a reignited passion for the Rocketown youth club I had started. We opened the new Rocketown club in downtown Nashville, complete with a huge performance area for weekly concerts and other special events, a coffee house, a skate park, and a small clothing store. Years earlier, we had lost our lease, and the reopening had been stalled as we struggled to raise funds, find a new building, and stay focused. It was a daunting task, but there was suddenly an urgency that this had to be done—and soon. I couldn't help but wonder, *If there had been a club like Rocketown in Littleton, Colorado, could it have reached those boys before they went on their bloody rampage?* Who knows? Maybe we could prevent some other kids with similar problems from turning to violence or ending their own lives.

DON'T BE AFRAID TO ASK FOR DIRECTIONS

That's when I got started. I enlisted the help of former President George Bush, Sr., and we went on the warpath. I was determined to fight for this thing. And it worked. I really believe all of that happened as a result of Columbine—and as a result of me asking some hard questions and being willing to act.

For some people, it may not be that clear. Something happens, maybe it was September 11th or a tragedy in your own family, and you feel changed. But where do you go from there? You don't have to open a youth facility to make a difference, but, as I've encouraged you throughout this book, be open to what God has for you to accomplish. We all have something to give. At the same time, don't be afraid to dream big. Everyday, people who imagined something huge and then worked hard to see it through have accomplished some amazing things.

Whatever your goals, as you get started, remember to apply what we've talked about earlier in this book. Obviously, you want to pray and seek the Lord about all the possibilities, checking in with Him about everything you're supposed to be doing—and not doing. He'll make it clear. Then talk to others about your plans. I have an accountability group that I bounce things off of, especially the big stuff. It consists of godly friends and mentors who know me well and can give me honest, fair feedback. I'm the first to admit, this can get difficult when what they have to say isn't what I want to hear. Who wants to be told no? But I know that I need to listen no matter what.

Finally, don't forget to ask for your own advice. It may sound a little silly, but deep down in your heart, you usually have a sense of what's right for you, and you'll be able to tell when you don't feel completely comfortable about pursuing a certain path. After years of growing and learning, I know that inside of me I have a fairly good guiding compass that directs me toward what I'm supposed to do. There's nothing mystical about it. It's just the Lord. And I can promise you that as you continue to walk with Him through the years, your sense of what's right and what's wrong gets sharpened. It gets easier the more you do it. The more you know yourself, the more you know God and know who you are in Him, the better you get at reading the signals.

YIELD

What signals has God been sending you? Have you been missing certain signs or maybe ignoring others? What choices have you made even though you knew in your heart they probably weren't the right ones? Is there a way you can make that right now, even after the fact? What choices have you made that were a result of listening to God and the good advice of Christian friends? How did that feel?

EVERYDAY EXTREMES

While we've been talking a lot about extreme cases in this chapter, about making the ultimate sacrifice and being asked to give up your life for what you believe, chances are you'll never face that kind of decision. But as you continue to grow in your faith, there will probably be other sacrifices you will be asked to make. Maybe you've already faced some of those tough decisions and know all too well what I'm talking about.

Have you ever had to distance yourself from a group of friends that was continually dragging you down instead of lifting you up? Maybe they were always gossiping or using language you found objectionable, and instead of being able to influence them positively, you felt they were beginning to affect you negatively. Did you ever find yourself not being able to join in the conversation about the latest video game, movie, or TV show because you opted not to play it, see it, or watch it due to some questionable content?

These can be tough choices to make, especially when the immediate result is that you're sitting home on a Saturday night or those around you are having more fun and seemingly suffering no bad consequences from their less-than-virtuous decisions. There's no doubt about it, sin can be enjoyable—for a season. If the things we weren't supposed to do held no real appeal, we would never be tempted. Instead, it would be easy to walk away and to always do the right thing. Unfortunately, since that first bite of fruit in the garden of Eden, we've been pulled in two different directions.

That's why when you do take a stand, you may find you're doing it all by yourself. This could seem like a pretty lonely place to be, but that doesn't mean it isn't the *right* place for you to be. In fact, that may just be a sign you're on the right track. After all, if everyone were standing up, there wouldn't be any need for you to. There wouldn't be a problem in the first place. But when you do find yourself feeling alone, you can take comfort in the fact that you're actually in good company. Some of the Bible's most godly men and women were often alone in doing what they believed was right.

Think about it. Job's friends tried to get him to blame God for his troubles instead of congratulating him for standing strong in his faith. Joseph's brothers threw him in a pit and left him for dead, in part because they were jealous of the plans they knew God had for him. But Job and Joseph stood firm, and you can, too.

And when you do, you'll never truly be alone. God will always be there with you.

NO TIME LIKE THE PRESENT

Most teenagers have had an adult at one time or another tell them, "These are the best years of your life!" You probably rolled your eyes after hearing this not-so-helpful message. I know I'd be tempted to. Between tough teachers and tougher tests, finding someone to sit with in the cafeteria, and hoping no one finds out about your secret crush, the teen years can feel a bit like one of those reality show physical challenges, only you never reach the finish line.

Whether these years are the happiest or the most difficult of your life, one thing is true of them for everyone: this is the time when you have some of the best opportunities to make the most of every minute. There aren't mortgages to pay and retirement accounts to fund and multiple bills screaming for your attention. You don't have family responsibilities to worry about or kids who need braces, new basketball shoes, or a costly college education. Your life is your own, despite what it may sometimes feel like.

So instead of counting the days until starting college or getting your own apartment or meeting that special someone, why not focus on making the most of the time you have right now? The Bible warns adults not to look down on you because of your youth. So you see, God knows you can accomplish amazing things, even before you're old enough to get a diploma or a driver's license. Your story is just beginning to be written. How will your chapters read when everything is said and done?

look for the signs

There are many events that have changed the course of my life. Columbine is only one of them. Were you one of those people who always thought there would be plenty of time to do everything you wanted to do? Are you feeling more of an urgency now to get busy? I sure hope so, and I look forward to hearing someday about the wonderful things you were able to accomplish by living each day as if it were your last.

what events have had an impact on you, causing you to reexamine your relationship with god? what would you do today if it were your last day on earth?

chapter six

Breakdown

Every era shapes human history. The events of the times have an impact on who we are and where we're headed. These may come in the form of positive changes that move us forward as a nation or as a civilization. (Certainly there are inventions you're thankful for: indoor plumbing, computers, air conditioning, surround sound, iPods?) There are also negative changes that can move us in a dangerous direction.

That's what I felt was happening in the mid-'90s. Our country was changing, and not for the better it seemed to me. As I watched the news or scanned the headlines in the morning newspaper, my heart sank. It looked like we were spiraling down big time in terms of our morality, and I wasn't the only one who thought so. Many of us were asking, "What's happening?" In answer to that question, I felt the need to sound some sort of warning call. Not that I thought I could completely turn things around with just a song, but I still felt like I had to stand up and say something, to call attention to the problem, before things got any worse.

The result was "Breakdown," a song I penned with my frequent writing partner, Wayne Kirkpatrick. It's a tune that, a decade later, I still think is relevant and a message we continually need to hear. In it, one of the topics I tackle is the lack of obligations or responsibility in today's age of "anything goes" sexuality.

If you're to believe TV, everyone is sexually promiscuous, moving from one relationship to another with few consequences and no commitment. Couples live together now with alarming frequency and not much thought at all to the long-term effects. It may be called *free love,* a term left over from the hippie movement of the late '60s and early '70s, but trust me, there is a price to be paid for giving away your heart (and your body) again and again.

Even some of our heroes, those we thought we could look up to—politicians, pro athletes, schoolteachers—have let us down. In the past few years, we've watched as representatives from each of these professions have appeared in high profile trials, forced to pay financial and criminal consequences for their sexual misconduct. Not to mention some celebrities, who, while we knew weren't all necessarily role models, seem to have sunk to even lower lows in their very public personal lives.

Not that you can't admire a basketball player solely for his jump shot or give a singer credit simply for her amazing vocal range. But be careful you're not also condoning the way that athlete mistreats women or the outfits that singer chooses to wear to flaunt her size-two body. It's hard to find role models today on TV's music channels or in the locker room. They exist, but they usually aren't the ones who wind up on the cover of *Sports Illustrated* or who find their videos in heavy rotation. Some even see less success *because of* their strong morals.

If a music artist isn't willing to show enough skin or date high-profile "bad boys" to get her picture in print, her career can suffer. It's the same for actors. Those who hop from bed to bed, appear with a new girl or guy on their arm each week, and hit all the raucous parties are the ones who get the publicity. Even athletes can be rewarded for their bad behavior. Just look at any number of professional athletes and their long list of big-money endorsements, and you know that's true.

We need to be careful who we put up on a pedestal these days. Of course, no one is perfect, and we shouldn't expect them to be, but I do wish the standards of those in the spotlight were a bit higher. Still, there are heroes to be found. Look around in your neighborhood, your school, your church, your family. They might be closer than you think.

YIELD

Who do you look up to? Whose pictures are hanging on your bedroom wall right now? Are they worthy role models or do you excuse their character because they possess other talents you admire? Who are moral role models for you? Do you even know what those you look up to believe about today's moral issues?

IN OURSELVES WE TRUST

"Breakdown" isn't just about our moral decline, but our spiritual one as well. Within its verses, I also talk about our country's changing attitude toward God's sovereignty and leadership. It's really no surprise that God's role in our nation continues to shrink considering we've become a people interested in meeting our own individual needs, whose main concern often seems to be "what's in it for me?"

While our Pledge of Allegiance still includes the line, "one nation, under God," the phrase "one nation, *over* God" is probably more accurate. Many Americans seem determined to put themselves first and God second . . . or third or fourth. For some, His name doesn't make it on the list at all. Debates continue to rage over whether or not it's constitutional to publicly display the Ten Commandments or to pray in school, and some political activists and politicians work overtime to twist and warp the Founding Fathers' original intentions, turning our constitutional guarantee of freedom of religion into a freedom *from* religion. That was never the way it was supposed to be.

FIGHTING THE GOOD FIGHT

Unfortunately, since I began singing "Breakdown" ten years ago, the problems haven't changed all that much. We're still struggling to regain our moral compass, and I think we're going to have to fight to the bitter end. Of course, everyone's idea of how to fight this moral decline is different. For me, I don't choose to stand out in front of an abortion clinic and wave a sign. I'm not going to start a mass boycott of a specific laundry detergent, sending out urgent e-mail messages asking everyone I know to do the same.

So how do I fight it? I think in my case it's more about living the life; it's about my everyday actions as I move through my world. I believe it's important for me to be aware—and then to also be willing to be corrected when I forget to remain watchful. A recent trip to the mall provided a perfect example.

I went out and bought a pair of new jeans, and my wife got upset with me. It's not that the purchase was too expensive. Instead, she took issue with the store I bought the pants from. To lure in young buyers, they use very suggestive advertising campaigns that feature a lot more skin than the clothing they're trying to sell. Having seen the images, I can't argue with her. She doesn't want to support that company in any way, and I agree with her. But to me, they were just a pair of jeans.

YIELD

What moral issues do you think are worth fighting for? What limits are put on what you watch, read, listen to, or wear? Were those boundaries set by Mom or Dad or are you responsible for making those choices yourself?

SOMEBODY'S WATCHING YOU

It was a good reminder to be more careful and to remember that I'm setting an example. Someone's always waiting to say, "Well, if *he* thinks it's okay, then I can do it, too." That's another reason why I'm usually very careful in deciding what I'm going to watch, read, listen to—even wear.

I'm not the only one setting an example, though. It's true that because I'm on stage or have my picture appear in magazines it may be easier for people to see me as a role model or to scrutinize my choices. But we're all setting an example with our lives, with both the good and the bad choices we make. Whether you're a pop star, a politician, or a pizza delivery guy, there are always eyes watching what you do. So be aware and remain vigilant. Make clear decisions about what you will and won't do and then live them out.

In my life, I regularly choose not to participate in things that are unhealthy, whether it's what I watch or eat or listen to. Setting those types of boundaries leads to specific choices for me. Will I see that movie? Buy that CD? Shop at that store? While your standards are hopefully similar (since we're both basing them on the Bible and the guidelines it gives us for living godly lives), the specific choices you make will probably be different. That's okay. We will each come to somewhat different conclusions about what specifically is and isn't appropriate for us.

One way you can be reasonably sure you're making informed decisions is to keep up with what's going on in the world around you. While you may choose not to condone or participate in certain things, it may still be necessary to know about them. That doesn't mean you need to watch twelve hours' worth of MTV's Spring Break coverage to know it's crossing the line of good taste. Instead, focus on getting the facts and try to stay up-to-date on the issues. I'm not encouraging you to sit around clutching the remote until you become a CNN junkie or learn to love C-Span. But you can't make informed decisions if you don't know what's going on.

YIELD

How aware are you of the world around you? What can you do to become more informed? Is there a current events class at school you could sign up for? Is there a daily newspaper lying around the house that you could look at for more than the sports scores or movie times?

LOSING THE BATTLE, WINNING THE WAR

I need to warn you: taking a good, hard look at the world around you can have serious side effects. Sometimes all that knowledge can be depressing. The more you learn, the more convinced you could become that we're fighting a losing battle. Abortion, divorce, teen pregnancy, political and corporate corruption . . . they're everywhere. But I believe that by standing up and being heard, we really *are* making a difference.

Even if we can't turn the tide completely or inspire huge changes, there are times when you are backed up against a wall so far that you say, "I have to stand up and speak my mind about this" or "I need to stand my ground." If we don't ever stand up for what's right (or point out what's wrong), we're going to find that people will begin to run all over us. Our views won't be heard and our opinions will no longer matter. In contrast, when we take that stand, no matter how far things have gone, I really do believe we're making a difference.

While it's easy to focus on all that's negative in our world, I see positive signs all the time. Press-wise, we always hear about the bad stuff going on. There's a disturbing saying in the news business: "If it bleeds, it leads." That means the bloodier the story, the more loss of life it involves, the better coverage it will get, either early in the newscast or on the front page of the paper. With that kind of mentality, it's no wonder we don't really hear a whole lot of good news.

That doesn't mean there aren't a lot of really great things going on. I hear stories every day about people making a difference in their communities, people starting much-needed new ministries, people reaching out to the orphans and widows around them as the Bible instructs them to do. For me, I get really encouraged when I hear about somebody's life being changed.

There are a lot of great things going on out there. As much as it may seem like we're falling apart as a country, there are plenty of positive things to point to that I feel very good about. So don't give up just yet. I don't think we're going down the tubes anytime soon.

We still need to remain on guard. There are those who aren't encouraged by those positive stories. Instead, they want to do us harm and distort the Gospel. That point was driven home on September 11th, and we continue to see battles fought around the globe over religion and moral issues. All this turmoil has caused some people to be more vocal about their faith, to think about the choices they were making and change their course. Others discovered a personal relationship with God for the first time in the aftermath of that horrible tragedy. But even as I write this, our country is still fighting a war. We have men and women overseas in foreign lands, risking their lives to protect us from those who want nothing more than to hurt us—supposedly in the name of religion.

Those battles won't be resolved anytime soon. This is a war that we're going to have to continue to fight. There is a lot of evil out there—both inside and outside America's borders. Some of it comes in the form of our own nation's moral decline. Other forms of evil are more obvious, using bombs and guns.

We have a lot to be optimistic about, but we need to also be on our guard against the forces of evil in any form. And when we see them, we need to be willing to stand up and speak out. One voice can make a difference. It has in the past when it came to injustices like slavery or racism. When it happens again, will you be ready?

There is a lot that is broken about America, but it's not beyond repair. A large share of the responsibility for leading us down the path of moral decline has to rest on the shoulders of popular culture. What part does it play in your life? Do you turn to TV and magazines to tell you how you ought to look? Do you buy into the airbrushed images they're selling, or do you get your value and self-worth from who you are in Christ? One thing I can say with certainty: you need to determine what you stand for before you're faced with a certain situation. If there's no rule, it's impossible to break it—and much easier to end up someplace you don't want to be.

what standards do you use to determine your morals and values? Do you look to your friends and popular culture to lead the way or do you make up the rules as you go along? what standards, morals, or values should you begin reshaping today?

chapter seven

Love Me Good

Do you think God has a sense of humor? I know He does. Just take a look at the platypus or the anteater and then try to convince me otherwise. Some people would like us to believe that we should only talk about God in hushed tones and that there's no place for humor or fun within the confines of Christianity.

I agree that religion is no laughing matter, and when we speak of God, the Creator of this vast and wonderful universe, it should be with awe and reverence. But I don't believe we need to be serious all the time to show our devotion. Sometimes this world is downright goofy, and it would be silly of us to pretend it wasn't.

Personally, I love to laugh. It lifts my spirits. It makes me feel better. It takes my mind off other weightier stuff. And why wouldn't it? It says right there in Proverbs 17:22 that "a cheerful heart is good

YIELD

Why do you think God made us with a sense of humor? Why is it important to be able to laugh? Are you someone who is able to laugh at yourself? When was the last time you laughed?

medicine." Life can be difficult enough sometimes without feeling like we have to be serious every single minute, and laughter can certainly lighten the load. Even the writer of Ecclesiastes knew that, saying in chapter 3 of that book that "there is a time for everything, and a season for every activity under heaven . . . a time to tear down and a time to build, a time to weep and a time to laugh, a time to mourn and a time to dance."

Did you see it there on the list? "A time to laugh." It's even biblical! Everything has its place, and laughter has a large place in my life. It even has a place in my music. I've written my share of songs about life's more serious moments, and I sing them regularly, thankful for the impact God allows them to have in the lives and hearts of those who hear them. But I also believe Christian musicians can have a sense of humor. I was certainly going for the lighter side of life when I recorded "Love Me Good," another song I wrote with Wayne. You can't sing a song with lines in it about Mongolian barbecue, the Brady Bunch, and Genghis Khan and expect it to be taken too seriously.

Give it a listen, and you know that this tune was meant to be fun. It's one of those songs that's just quirky, and I love performing it live. And I can't find a single thing wrong with that. Why does everything have to be so serious all the time? Why can't we just lighten up?

Of course, not everyone shares my sense of humor. There are a lot of people who love that song and others who just don't like it or don't get it. Even though it was a #1 hit on Christian radio and I was invited to open up the Dove Awards with the song that year, according to the Gospel Music Association's definition, "Love Me Good" didn't meet their criteria for what constitutes a "Christian" song. That meant we could perform it at the awards ceremony to entertain the crowd, but it couldn't actually be nominated for an award. That's just one more strange and funny twist in the story of this not-so-serious song.

While I believe "Love Me Good" was an appropriate use of humor, there are times when it's just not right to try to be funny. Like the verse in Ecclesiastes says, "There is a time for everything." We've all been in youth group or a class at school when someone was using humor to get attention or distract from what someone else was saying. In that case, it's disruptive and annoying. It can even be downright rude. Some people also enjoy getting a laugh at someone

YIELD

What do you personally find funny that maybe others don't? Have there been times when you used humor when it wasn't appropriate? Did someone get hurt? How did you feel afterward?

else's expense. That kind of behavior may get you the attention you were seeking, for a moment at least, but it will also get you branded as someone who's willing to hurt others for his own gain. That kind of label isn't going to win you any true friends in the long run.

MORE THAN MEETS THE EYE

Whatever other people's opinions are about "Love Me Good," I enjoy the song, just singing some of those crazy lines. More importantly, I know that hidden within that happy-go-lucky tune is a message we all really need to hear.

It's no big secret that we all want to be loved. More than that, we *need* to be loved. We're programmed for it. There's even research to prove it. Studies have shown that when babies aren't held, cuddled, or shown affection in their first weeks or months of life, they can suffer not just psychological but actual physical consequences. It can affect their ability to gain weight and their development. In the most extreme cases, they can fail to thrive. And while we may outgrow many things from our younger years—from cribs to clothes to our need to sleep with the light on—we never outgrow our need to be loved.

Knowing we need love and asking for it are two different things. You're not going to walk up to someone and start singing "Love Me Good." Sometimes it can be hard, though, to admit the thing our heart wants most. Love is a difficult thing to ask for. What if we get rejected?

The reason we may have such a hard time expecting love from those around us is that we struggle with whether or not we deserve to be loved in the first place—especially the way God loves us, with His unconditional love. Unfortunately, the way we're loved in this world isn't always a great reflection of God's kind of no-matter-what love. That's where it gets confusing.

I personally wrestled with my own worthiness when I was younger because there was a lot of legalism in the church I grew up in. While the Bible was filled with talk about love and forgiveness, it was pretty evident that in this congregation if you did certain things, you were automatically on the blacklist. As a result, the message came through loud and clear: you'd better watch your step. That type of rigid atmosphere takes its toll. For me, it meant I never really knew about unconditional love until I was in my late teens. It was then that I had a sort of spiritual reawakening, and I rededicated my life.

YIELD

Have you ever wondered why God bothers to love you? Have you ever doubted that He could really love someone like you as much as the Bible says He does? What effects do you think that has on your faith? On your ability to trust God with every area of your life?

ACCEPTING THE GIFT

Not that my struggle to believe God loves me no matter what was over from that day forward. It's an ongoing battle, one that the devil hopes we lose. I think that is the enemy's main purpose: he sets out to discourage us, using our weakness to make us feel unworthy. So we continue to beat ourselves up. We know the truth, but it's amazing how we can still be sucked in, how he can make us start to wonder, *Why would God ever love someone like me?*

You may feel that way in your heart, but don't forget what you know in your head. The Bible is clear: God loves each of us because we are His. We were created in His image, and He's written His name on each of our hearts. There's nothing you have to do to earn that love, and there's nothing you can do to make Him love you more—or less. Even if you were the only person on earth, He still would have sent His Son to die for you alone. You're that important to Him! It can be a bit overwhelming to hear those things, but it's true. God really does love you that much. No matter what you've done, what you've thought about doing, what you might do in the future, He loves you.

The message does eventually sink in for most of us. I can honestly say that I think I really, really know better today than ever before the true, unconditional love of God. And that one thing makes all the difference in my life. I sleep better. I'm at peace. I'm happy. There's a lot of joy in my life. I feel like I'm more productive.

While those benefits are great, it's not just about me. Refusing to accept God's gift of unconditional love takes its toll on those around you. If you say you're a believer but you don't believe God loves you the way the Bible promises He does, it colors everything you do. You can't give as much, you can't do as much, until you really come to terms with this. Now that I have, I think I extend more mercy. I feel like I'm more forgiving. And that affects those around me in a positive way. All the things that you hope to be start to rise to the top. That kind of amazing love, when you really, truly get it, makes you want to love others the same way.

YIELD

When you think about God's unconditional love for you, what do feel? Happy? Grateful? Unworthy? Which of those emotions do you think are from God? How do you want others to feel when you give them a gift? Now how do you think God wants you to feel about the gift He's given you?

GETTING AND GIVING

You may have already guessed that "Love Me Good" isn't as much about God's love for us as it is about how we're supposed to love others—and how we're not. The Bible is pretty clear about how we're to treat those around us. We're literally commanded in Leviticus 19:18 to "love your neighbor as yourself." And in the New Testament, love is mentioned again and again. The most famous passage is probably 1 Corinthians 13, which tells us in detail just exactly what love is. In case you need a reminder, patient and kind make the list, while proud, rude, easily angered, and self-seeking are held up as examples of what love isn't. We're also told that love "always protects, always trusts, always hopes, always perseveres. Love never fails."

That's a tall order to fill. Are you up to the challenge? Well, some Bible teachers say you can boil down what God wants from us into one simple sentence: Love the Lord your God with all your heart, mind, and soul, and love your neighbor as yourself. (Mark 12:30–31)

YIELD

How do you define love? How do you show love to your family and friends? Does it fit the description given in 1 Corinthians 13? Who are the "neighbors" in your life? Could they be the person who has a locker next to yours, the student in that desk one row over, the kid on the bus who gets off at your stop? Are you loving them?

GIVING LOVE A BAD NAME

"Love Me Good" is also aimed at those who are currently loving others badly. It's a message directed at that person who feels the need to make everything into an issue. Or maybe it's talking to someone who's negative all the time. We all know someone like that and how that kind of attitude can spill over onto everyone around them. Or the song could be sung to that somebody who's always dealing with something, who thrives on continually being in crisis mode. The song is a reminder that those people don't have to always take life so seriously. There's nothing wrong with having a good time.

Not everyone gets the message, and I feel sorry for those people who don't. I see them all the time, and they're miserable.

Sometimes it's something carried over from childhood. While I was raised in a positive, Christian home with a mom and dad who always loved me unconditionally, that's not the case for everyone. I see so many young people in the church whose dad left when they were little or maybe their mom doesn't really care about them and they are deeply affected by it. They can't love other people well because they feel like they haven't been loved well themselves.

I hurt for those people, but it can be hard for me to know how to help in these types of situations because these are issues I'm not familiar with. I didn't grow up dealing with that. But it doesn't mean I'm helpless. Instead, I'm careful to explain that while I can't empathize or know exactly what they're feeling, I can sympathize with them and provide a listening ear or a shoulder to cry on. I can also pray with them and bathe them in scriptures, praying specific verses just for them. I can be a friend, and in my own way I can "love them good."

For all I know, you personally have a dark cloud that hangs over you because you have a skewed image of love. Maybe you've been hurt in the past by someone you trusted. It could be that a parent or relative, someone who was supposed to love you and care for you, dropped the ball and didn't fulfill that responsibility.

I hate to hear those stories, and they really are tragic. But no matter how you've been loved (or not loved, as the case may be) on this earth, you can take comfort in the fact that we're all loved equally well by God. While it can seem easier to wallow in your pain and rehash what you missed out on in the past, God wants you to focus on the future and the love you're called to show to others.

We've been given the greatest gift imaginable, and we're asked to pass a little of it on, to love others because He's loved us. That shouldn't be that hard to do, when you really think about it. After all, when you discover a great new ice cream flavor or exercise routine or clothing store, your excitement bubbles over and, before you know it, you're telling everyone you know. How much more excited should you be, then, when you discover how much God really loves you? If you're like me, you'll be practically bursting with joy. And then the problem won't be how to start loving others "good," it will be that you won't be able to stop.

Love is a huge theme throughout the Bible and in our lives as well. The radio is continuously cranking out songs about love, books are filled with stories about it, and countless hours are spent dreaming of finding that one true love. There are even Web sites devoted to pairing singles into couples, and before you start to laugh, you should know they're becoming a big business.

There's nothing wrong with romantic love and wanting to experience that in your life, but before "you" become a "we," make sure you've spent plenty of time learning what love really is. Practice loving others well in a non-romantic way, and you'll be more prepared to handle that other kind of love when it comes along.

So where do you start? Why not try taking a look at those closest to you? Are your interactions with your parents and siblings a testament to the kind of love we've talked about in this chapter? What about the way you treat your friends? Your teachers or youth leaders? Are there other people in your life that God wants you to show some love to today?

chapter eight

Cry for Love

No. It's something none of us like to hear. But we do hear it. That ugly little one-syllable, two-letter word comes at us from our parents, our teachers, our government, and even from our God. Sometimes we hear it so often, it seems like there's no other word in the English language (see, there it is again in this sentence!). It's never fun to be told that we can't have something we want or that we can't do something we've been looking forward to. But usually when we hear no, as much as I hate to admit this, it's for our own good.

From the time we're toddlers, our parents have to continually tell us no to protect us from danger or harm and to keep us happy and healthy. "No, you can't climb on that." "No, don't stick that in the electrical outlet." "No, you can't stay up instead of taking a nap." As we start school, the limits continue. We can't watch too much TV, we can't walk home from the bus stop alone, and we can't head outside without coats or gloves in the winter. As we enter the teen years, the rules are just beginning. Bedtime, curfew, music, meals. We're ready to start making some decisions about what's best for us, but our parents may have other ideas. Still, no matter how strict Mom and Dad are, this is the time when we begin to learn to say no for ourselves.

Don't say no to staying up too late, and you'll learn pretty fast that you can't stay awake in class the next day and your grades will suffer. Don't say no on a regular basis to high-fat snacks or the school cafeteria's daily pizza offering, and you'll soon learn you don't fit into any of your clothes. Through trial and error, you begin to see that saying no at times is a necessity.

YIELD

Has there been a time when you were told no only to see later how that protected you from something bad? What would have happened if you had been told yes? What limits do you currently set and which ones are still up to Mom and Dad? When was the last time you said no to yourself? Was it hard to do?

Sometimes, it's even necessary to say no to good things. This is where it can get complicated. Choosing not to listen to an objectionable CD or not to go to a party where you know there may be underage drinking going on is one thing, but saying no to something positive can be really hard.

So why do it, you're probably asking? Just because something isn't obviously bad for you, that doesn't mean it's something you should do. There may be times when you need to pass on an opportunity because you're overcommitted or because it's not something you're called to. Sometimes you may not even know why you feel like you should say no, but you've prayed about it and just don't feel like God is leading you to say yes. That's reason enough right there. Saying yes for the wrong reasons can be much worse than saying no for the right ones.

THE DANGERS OF BEING A "YES" MAN

A few years back, I learned the hard way what can happen when you aren't willing to say no enough. Life was moving way too fast. Forget taking time to stop and smell the flowers, I didn't even have time to give them a sniff as I blew by at lightning speed. I was burned out and in danger of having a nervous breakdown.

How did I get to this point? The problem was, I just didn't know how to say no. It took me a long time to accept that there are limits to what I can do. There were so many good opportunities coming my way, so many people who seemed to need my help, that it felt wrong to turn them down.

So I didn't.

"Yeah, I'll help you with that ministry." "Yeah, I'll do that benefit." "Yeah, I'll do that, plus tour, plus raise a family, plus have a spiritual life." All that activity almost brought my life to a screeching halt. I was at the end of my rope. That's when I finally listened to my mentor Don Finto who assured me that it really is okay to say no. Accepting that and applying it has changed my life.

This isn't a problem that's unique to artists who spend a good deal of time on the road, though. Any of us can get off track. It's part of the price we pay for living in America. There are so many opportunities here and so many options that what should be a blessing often becomes a curse. Instead of enjoying some of those possibilities, we don't want to miss out on anything. We're the first in line and the last one to leave, hoping to drink up as much of life as we possibly can. And you don't need me to tell you this, but living that way is just downright unhealthy.

Don't fool yourself, either, into thinking you're simply making the most of every moment. If you're cramming in so much that you're exhausted, overwhelmed, or are letting priorities like faith and family slide, then something's out of balance. Making the most of every moment and running yourself into the ground are two totally different things.

YIELD

What have you said yes to in the past when you should have said no? What were the results? What is currently on your plate that shouldn't be? Is there a way that you can responsibly go about changing that?

THE DANGERS OF PEOPLE PLEASING

I probably took years off my life before I learned to say no. I was running so hard in all kinds of different directions that I'm lucky I survived it at all. I remember thinking I could potentially have a heart attack, and that woke me up. I don't allow myself to get overcommitted now, and not just for health reasons. More than anything, I just know it's the right thing to do. Also, I don't want to go back again. Once you get to that place a few times, where you're drowning in too much to do, you realize that whatever you have to do to not feel like that again, you'll do it.

Thank God I realized what a trap saying yes can be, and I determined that I don't want to live that way. I want to be free to take time for hanging out in my backyard or walking on the farm or just being quiet. That's how we refuel, and the lack of that kind of downtime is how I had found myself running on empty. But not anymore. This is a lesson that has stuck with me.

I have never forgotten how overwhelmed I felt during that frantic time, though, teetering on the edge of a breakdown. Maybe that's why, when I sat down soon after that period in my life to write with Nashville songwriter Brent Bourgeois, I knew I wanted to tackle it in a song. Soon after, "Cry for Love" was born. It's a testament to taking on too much, and crying out to God while you're in the middle of it all.

Still, it took some practice to utter the word *no* at first. I'm a real people pleaser by nature, and I love making people happy, so telling them I couldn't do something didn't feel good. But I finally learned I'm not doing anybody any favors if I don't take care of myself. Keep that up, and I'd have nothing left to give anyone.

Over the years, it's become easier to say no and mean it. In fact, I'm probably in better shape than I ever have been in terms of saying no and feeling okay, whatever the fallout. And there will be fallout, I guarantee you. While I know I'm making the right choice for me, the reality is that there are times when someone is not going to understand or somebody's going to be upset. Some people will think I'm not sensitive to their needs or others might imagine my no has less to do with making smart-but-tough choices and more to do with the fact that they think I've developed a big head. And the negative reactions go on and on.

How do I handle responses like that? I admit they can be kind of hurtful at first, especially because I know my heart. But then I remember that ultimately I don't answer to man, I answer to God, and one day I'm going to have to give Him an account for how well I managed the life He gave me to lead. That's the bottom line.

Fortunately, it gets easier as you get older (and, hopefully, wiser). Also, that old adage "practice makes perfect" definitely applies here. The more you do it, the less trouble you'll have recognizing when saying no is the right thing and, even more importantly, when it's what God wants you to do.

In those earlier days, I used to be so in the middle of it, always second-guessing and wondering, *Should I do this? Should I not do this?* These days, I'm finding that my yeses are "yes" and my nos are "no." I don't waver nearly so much once I've made a decision. I'm more definitive and sure about what I'm supposed to say—whether it's no or yes—and how I'm supposed to respond.

Once I do that, I can feel okay about it and not lose any sleep. If you've never been there, if you're still drowning in a sea of over-commitment or taking on responsibilities because you feel guilty instead of called, you need to give it a try. It's really a wonderful place to be.

SAYING NO FOR NOW

One thing I've learned that can make saying no easier is that sometimes you're just saying no for now. You're not ruling out the possibility of ever getting involved; you're simply recognizing that this isn't what you're called to do at this particular moment in time. Don't get me wrong: I'm not saying it still won't be hard to pass up certain things, especially when you're talking about something you really want. But timing really is everything, and when you try to rush God, you rarely get the result you were after in the first place.

Learning to say no for now also means you will have time to do what you are called to do really well. For me, that meant I first had to discover I wasn't Superman. (This may have been obvious to you, but for me it was a revelation.) I thought I was. And I thought I could do all these different things that I had my hands in at the same time and it would be okay. I couldn't. Not if I wanted to do them well, anyway.

As a result, I asked God what it was that I really was supposed to be doing and decided to focus on that. Instead of having my hand in six or seven things and doing each of them just okay, I wanted to work hard at doing a few things and doing them well.

In my life, right now, one of those things I need to focus on is my family. That's the biggest priority. After that, what I feel I'm really called to is what I do for a living: make music. And I know I can't make the best music I'm capable of unless I'm saying no in some other areas of my life, so I do that. I'm not going to be able to go out and be very productive on this next project if I'm running around trying to do all this other stuff. I say no to that stuff so that I can say yes to what God has called me to focus on in this chapter of my life.

I've said no so well that I got to a point where I didn't have one engagement—not one concert, not one benefit, not one public appearance—on the schedule for six months. It left me free to concentrate on making my next record, and that felt great. I think it'd been fifteen years since I had a clean slate like that, for six months with nothing on the books, and it wasn't easy to make it happen. It meant I had to go to my management company and say, "Guys, I feel like God is calling me to shut it down completely." That meant I had to say no to playing at a local hockey game even though my manager is friends with the coach. It meant I had to say no to other good opportunities that were things I could really get excited about. But I knew it was the right thing for that time.

In the past, recording has often been done in the midst of distractions. Not that I don't feel like I made some really good music in the middle of all that, but there has always been something hanging over my head; there was always an activity or event lurking around the corner, and each of those things required shifting gears. After more than twenty years of doing this, though, I've finally learned that making a record is enough to have on my to-do list at one time.

Of course, you may not be able to pull the plug on all your other activities to focus on one thing. Don't worry; it's likely that you're not called to. The main point is to tune in to what thing or things God has for you to do, and focus on that. Often, we say yes to something out of guilt or a misguided sense of obligation. The more you can hone in on what you're called to do, the easier it will be to say no to what you're not.

Keep in mind, it took me years of doing too much before I made a change. Even now, it's still a bit of trial and error. That means that chances are, even with the best of intentions, there will be times when you will find yourself in over your head. Don't worry, even if you feel you're in danger of going under for the third time. Help is close by. Just remember to ask for it. Adults in your life can give you advice on how to scale back so you can get back on track. Then try to learn something from the experience. How did you get there? How will you prevent it from happening next time? Most important, don't get too down on yourself. This is a process, and it's all part of learning how to become the person God wants you to be.

What if you become so careful about not doing too much, that you suddenly find that you're doing too little? That's a situation that's easy to fix. Go back to the beginning and look at your gifts —What are you good at? What do you feel called to?—then seek out opportunities to use them. Pray about it, ask friends and family for advice or input, and don't be shy about spreading the word that you have something to give. There's always plenty to be done, so chances are you won't be idle for long.

So much of our life is spent trying to find balance. We do too much or too little. In the teen years, it's hard not to get overcommitted because there are so many exciting new things to try. You try on different roles and identities and see what fits—and what doesn't. There's nothing wrong with sampling what's available, just try to look at each opportunity as a learning experience, teaching you something about who you are and who you're meant to be. And when you're done, don't forget to apply the lessons you've learned. Each experience can help bring you closer to your real calling and purpose.

As you explore what's out there, be realistic about your time and schedule. Keep your priorities in mind and remember that it's okay to say no to a lot of things so you can say yes to the important things. As you practice this, what are you learning about yourself? Does it get easier to say no as time goes on? What do you think God is trying to teach you by not always saying yes to your requests?

What Bible stories can you find where God said no to someone? What were the circumstances? And the results?

chapter nine

straight to the heart

We've all heard the expression "my heart just wasn't in it." Have you ever been involved in a project or an undertaking and the feeling just wasn't there? You probably couldn't even put your finger on what was missing from that particular scenario; you just knew that something was. It's a matter of chemistry. Who knows why we're drawn to certain things and not others, why we develop a crush on one person and not another, why a certain activity thrills us and another bores us to tears. It's another one of the wonderful mysteries of God's big, wide world.

For me, having my heart in something makes all the difference, although I admit I can't always predict what will grab me at first. I remember years ago when fellow musician Billy Sprague told me that some youth camp was using my song "Friends" as a theme song and that I should meet the camp director, a guy named Joe White. They wanted me to come to the camp and sing for them, but I distinctly remember I didn't want to go. There wasn't really any good reason for my reluctance. I just wasn't excited about trying to find the time in my already busy schedule to go to a camp.

As is often the case, God had other plans.

I ended up visiting Kanakuk Kamps—and I've been back every year since for nearly two decades. You'd have to go yourself to truly understand what I found there, but it was an amazing time. Maybe it was the kids or the excitement that was in the air. It was an adrenaline rush just to be a part of it. And it's not only a camp, it's the most amazing camp I've ever been to. Period.

You see what I mean about the heart? Mine is definitely in this ministry, and it makes all the difference when it comes to motivation. I don't have to psyche myself up to help out. I can't wait to get there and participate. I look forward to it.

YIELD

Where is your heart right now? What opportunities or activities make you excited to pitch in and help out? What do you like about them?

FRINGE BENEFITS

As if that weren't enough, I did meet Joe, just as my friend Billy suggested, and he hasn't just become one of my dearest friends, he's changed my life. From there, I started writing the camp's annual theme songs, several of which have ended up on my records. I believe the first one that I wrote was called "Take It to the Top," but the first one that made it onto a CD was "Love Crusade." You wouldn't know this, but it was originally called "Feed the Fire," to fit that summer's theme. Then we went back and changed the lyrics for the album. But one of my favorite theme songs that was later released as a single is "Straight to the Heart." It represents so much of what I love about Kanakuk and getting involved in ministries like it. Their direction is clear, and they continually point me and others back to the One who made our hearts in the first place.

Even as I write this, I'm working on coming up with a theme for this summer's program. Every year it always comes down to the wire, with me in the studio until 2 a.m. putting the finishing touches on the song before I have to FedEx it out to Joe the next morning. Despite the pressure, I love it.

I know what you're thinking: I've become pretty involved for someone who wasn't even interested in visiting the camp when I first heard about it. Well, you're right: I have, and I love it. Something about this particular program touched my heart, and I can't help but remain a part of this.

One of the draws for me is that Kanakuk is a sports camp, something I'm naturally interested in. Another irresistible aspect is their remarkable philosophy about how they love kids and teenagers. Some of the campers who arrive there have real problems, but Joe's philosophy is you can break a habit in twenty-one days, and he and his team work hard to help those who attend do just that. There's also Kids Across America, a non-profit organization that supports two camps that are devoted exclusively to inner-city kids. I've been involved in that for more than a decade now, and it's been great to watch the entire program grow. When I first stepped on the grounds, there were only two camps, but now there are eight or nine different camps in two different states.

You may not see what the big deal is, but for me Kanakuk is a way that I am able to give back and make a difference, an ideal that's been constant throughout my career. Sometimes I've really had to look to find places where I can do that. Other times, there are opportunities I've been naturally (or supernaturally?) drawn to. For some reason, God put Kanakuk on the map for me, for my life.

This makes sense since one of the greatest joys of my life is trying to find ways to give part of myself away. As I've grown older, I've really come to believe that's what it's all about. There are just certain things we're drawn to, and for me, I love pouring myself into that camp.

YIELD

What have you found to do that you can really put your whole heart into? How did you know it was the right fit for you? Were you reluctant in the beginning, like me, or was it an automatic slam-dunk?

One of the great things about this particular camp is that when I'm there, I'm just another camper. No one treats me like a celebrity. I'm allowed to become a kid, and I get as much out of the program as anybody else there. It's one place where I don't have the normal pressures on me, and that doesn't happen very often. No one asks for autographs (there's actually a rule against it). Joe and his staff make sure everyone understands "he's just one of us." I think it makes a difference for the campers as well because it's healthy for them to see I'm just a normal guy. Once I come down off that stage, I deal with the same issues they do, and I always have.

LOVE IN ANY LANGUAGE

Kanakuk isn't the only cause close to my heart. Compassion International, a child sponsorship agency that provides education, food, spiritual guidance, and other assistance to children in poorer areas around the world, is another organization that kind of snuck up on me. I was asked to be a spokesman, but I actually declined at first. I really believed in what they were doing, but I wanted to know more, so I said, "What I'd love to do is sponsor a kid."

They eagerly signed me up, and I wrote a monthly check to help a young girl in South America. The program impressed me, and it wasn't long before I told Compassion I wanted to see firsthand what they were doing. I wasn't going to sign on the dotted line to become more involved if I couldn't check it out for myself.

I had no idea what I was in for. I had been sponsoring young Gavi for less than a year when I boarded a plane bound for Ecuador, where she lived. I'll never forget the first time my sponsored child saw me. She came up and started crying, and she didn't let go of me for three days. A lot of that probably had to do with the fact that she didn't know her dad, and her mom left her when she was just two years old. At the time she was being raised by her grandparents, and I became this father figure in her life. Despite not speaking the language or understanding the culture, I was so drawn to this ministry.

My heart was so touched by what was being done that I went back eight or nine times throughout Gavi's childhood to see how she was progressing. She was just six or seven when I began sponsoring her, and three years ago, on my last trip to her home village, I was proud to present her with her high school diploma. It was the first time a guy had ever done that in her all-girls Catholic school! It was pretty cool.

That's the thing: you get involved to help others and find out the one who benefits the most is you.

I've been involved with Compassion now for at least fifteen years, and with Kanakuk for longer than that. That's long enough to really see God work in some amazing ways, to see the signs of His love for others and for me on a regular basis.

As you know, I need to be careful not to take on too much because I don't want to get overcommitted, but I know it's important to make sure I'm involved somewhere. I get hit up with stuff

YIELD

Have you ever done something to help someone else and found that you got much more out of it than that person did? Why do you think that is? Why is it that we get so much out of giving, something that's supposed to be for others and not ourselves?

all the time, but I feel like it's important to concentrate on a few things that I can really get involved in and do well. Compassion, Kanakuk, and Rocketown are those things for me—for now anyway. Who knows what God has waiting around the bend?

HAVE A HEART

God gave each of us a heart. It may not look anything like the cute Valentine's Day version that we see on cards and wrapped around chocolates to communicate romantic love, but it's there, beating away inside of you. While it's really no more than a complex pump, for some reason we seem to tie a lot of our feelings to this one mysterious organ. We believe that some people seem to have more heart than others, and people who are particularly compassionate we call "tenderhearted." When we want some sympathy or mercy we might ask someone to "have a heart." But really what we do for others, how caring we are to those around us, has nothing to do with aortas and ventricles. It has to do with how we respond to the love and mercy God has shown us and what He has called us to do as a result.

When you're young, love is often on your mind. Who will you fall in love with? What will it feel like? When will it happen? God wants our minds to be on love, and there's nothing wrong with the romantic kind, but what Jesus talks about most often in the New Testament is "agape" love. That's Greek for a more brotherly type of caring. No, it's not likely to inspire some new nighttime soap opera or a slew of reality shows, and it's not the kind of thing love songs are written about, but it's important nonetheless.

We've talked about how we're supposed to love our neighbor, but did you know that in 1 Corinthians 13:1–3, Paul tells us that we can do great things, amazing things, but if they're not done with the right motivation, they become worthless:

> If I speak in the tongues of men and of angels, but have not love, I am only a resounding gong or a clanging cymbal. If I have the gift of prophecy and can fathom all mysteries and all knowledge, and if I have a faith that can move mountains, but have not love, I am nothing. If I give all I possess to the poor and surrender my body to the flames, but have not love, I gain nothing.

It sounds like God doesn't want our body if our heart isn't part of the package.

IT ONLY TAKES A SPARK

Are you starting to get the message? Love is pretty powerful. It can transform our actions from lifeless to life changing. When there is love in whatever we do, it's contagious. It melts hard hearts and inspires others.

Why is God so worried about you showing love to others? After all, you're just one person, right? How much difference can you possibly make?

A lot.

We don't live in a vacuum. What we do affects those around us—for better or for worse. It's like one of those domino mazes where you knock one over and the rest come tumbling down after it. If you do something positive, it can trigger other positive acts. If you do something negative, unfortunately, the same thing happens in reverse. It's where we get the phrase "domino effect."

One way we have an impact is simply by sharing what's going on with us. Word of mouth is a powerful thing. By talking about my experiences with Compassion from the stage, we've found sponsors for more than 20,000 kids. I know I'm fortunate to have a built-in platform because of my music that gives me the opportunity to reach thousands of people at a time with a particular message. But you don't need to be on stage to have an impact. Do something small in your community, with love as the motivation, and others will take notice. Hopefully, it will motivate them to reach out to someone else in love. Soon, the dominoes will start falling, and who knows, they might never stop.

If you've ever sat through a sermon on tithing, you've probably heard the phrase "God loves a cheerful giver." That's not just about money, though. God doesn't just want your wallet, He wants your heart. While giving financially can be a great exercise in obedience,

YIELD

Is there a particular event or person whose loving actions inspired you? Maybe it was a news story you watched or an article you read about someone else reaching out with God's love. What did you do as a result? What can you do now?

giving of your time and of yourself is just as important. But whether it's money or time you're doling out, there has to be heart behind it. Some of us want to make loving others another thing to check off our to-do list. We're like the Pharisees of the New Testament, following God's rules to the letter, without any heart behind our "good" works. That's a sure way to be a clanging cymbal.

Put your heart into what you do, though, and you'll go from clanging cymbal to full symphony in no time. Whatever your gifts and level of ability, if love is your motivation, you'll always have plenty to give.

While I get so much out of giving and being involved with different ministries and causes, I get just as excited about encouraging others to use their gifts. While working with Rocketown is great, it's even more of a thrill to plug in others. I get such a kick out of helping them see their strengths and their unique gifts, and then turning them loose.

who has inspired you to use your gifts for others? How can you pass that on? Are there people you can help to discover their own gifts and talents and then encourage them to find a way to use them?

The Bible says, "For where your treasure is, there your heart will be also" (Luke 12:34). What do you treasure or value? How does that affect how you live your life and how you love others?

chapter ten

I'll Lead You Home

So your life is completely in order. You're spending regular time with God, you're making your faith a priority, and you're finding ways to give back some of what God has given to you by reaching out to others. Life should be great, right?

You would think. But you remember Job, don't you? A whole book of the Old Testament is devoted to his story, and it's not the most uplifting tale—at least in the beginning. The Bible says he was "blameless and upright" (wouldn't we all love for God to say that about us?), but by the end of Job chapter 1 his children are dead, his camels and sheep have been stolen, and his servants have been carried off or killed. Not exactly a story you'd use to sell people on the benefits of living the Christian life.

These calamities didn't all happen by accident, either. Satan saw that Job's faith was strong so he suggested that if this godly man's situation changed, he'd quickly turn from praising God to cursing Him. But even when he was covered with painful sores from head to toe, Job didn't give in. Things were so bad at one point that his wife encouraged him to go ahead and curse God and die, but Job replied, "You are talking like a foolish woman. Shall we accept good from God, and not trouble?" (Job 2:10).

Even in the midst of all his suffering, Job understood that God doesn't owe us anything. What Job had was God's to give, and it was also God's to take. He didn't worship God because of what He'd given him in this life (although he certainly enjoyed those things and was thankful). Instead, Job worshiped God because he knew it was what God deserved.

YIELD

What do you have to lose that would be the modern day equivalent of Job's servants and livestock? How would you respond if those things were suddenly taken away? Would you have the strength to keep praising God as Job did?

TESTING, 1, 2, 3, TESTING . . .

What does this have to do with you? Well, unfortunately, once you start doing the right things, making good choices, and actively looking for ways to grow in your faith and share it with others, you're a prime target for spiritual attack. True, you don't have a herd of camels to lose, but follow God long enough and there will be trials that test your faith. And these aren't the multiple-choice kind of tests that you can cram for the night before. I know. I've been there.

Not that I would compare any part of my journey to Job, but I can relate to some of the questioning he did, asking God what was going on. In 1995, I found myself asking some similar questions when I wound up in what I can only describe as a desert. I was in a spiritual funk, and try as I might, I just couldn't seem to snap out of it.

Now, I had read all about Job many times, and I knew of other more recent stories of good Christians going through bad times, so I was somewhat prepared. I knew deserts were a part of life. If we want the peaks, those great high points where we feel like we're invincible, we have to take the valleys as well. It's a package deal. So I was okay with visiting the desert, I just didn't want to live there. But as the months dragged on, I didn't see any end in sight.

Depression was a new thing for me, and I couldn't understand it. My family was fine. I was fine. It just didn't make sense. Worst of all, since I didn't know what brought it on, I didn't have any idea how to fix it. You start to wonder, *Is there something wrong with me?* But I knew I wasn't going crazy. I was sure it had to do with the spiritual world, that other world that I wish we could see. I was being attacked. I just didn't know why. And I couldn't figure out why it was taking so long to get through this. As a result, a lot of my prayers consisted of going, "God, deliver me. What are You trying to show me here? What am I doing wrong?" I was really struggling to figure it out.

Finally, after six months of waiting and wondering, I got up early one morning and drove to my recording studio. It's tucked away in an old house, and I knew it would be quiet there. It wasn't even light out yet when I arrived, but I made my way inside, went into my office, and I just lost it. Eventually I ended up at the piano, where I often turn when I don't know how else to express what I'm feeling, and the words "Leave it to Me; I'll lead you home" came to me. Suddenly, after months of praying and struggling, I felt like the Lord came and rescued me. On that morning, He pointed the way out of the desert, and that was when I started coming back.

YIELD

Have you ever found yourself in a spiritual desert, feeling far away from God and not sure why? When did it end and what brought that about? What did you learn from that time in your life?

Looking back, I still don't have many answers. I don't know what was different about that particular morning or why God chose then to deliver me. I just know that suddenly I wasn't under the water anymore. It was like I was healed, like I had been paralyzed and then I could suddenly walk. I was free. It was the wildest thing.

I'm also not sure exactly what God wanted me to learn from my time in the desert. I still look back on it and find that I'm not sure why it happened. I probably won't ever know, but I know what to do the next time I find myself in a similar situation. To get myself through, I quoted a lot of scripture, particularly the Psalms, in an effort to stay positive. I have a lot of them memorized and would repeat them to myself when I was feeling particularly low.

I would also pray scripture. There were times when that was really all I could do because I was so down I didn't know what else to say. It was something Don Finto had taught me one day when we were walking around Radnor Lake. He sat me down and started talking to me, but soon enough I realized he was really quoting Colossians. He had it memorized. The difference was, he was personalizing it, changing it so that is sounded as if Paul had written that letter directly to me. It blew my mind and I thought, *I have to learn how to do that!* Now keep in mind, I barely passed English in high school, and I still have to put cheat sheets on my piano when I play, so how was I going to memorize? Well, Don suggested I start with Colossians 1:9–16. I went home that night and stayed up until three o'clock in the morning and memorized it. Other passages followed. Psalm 139. Psalm 138. Romans 8. I did Colossians 1. I did Colossians 3. And I just started praying scripture. Little did I know how helpful it would be to me down the road.

To me, there's nothing better than praying scripture. It's very affirming. You can be in the lowest funk of all, and you read certain parts of scripture and it's impossible for it not to make you feel better. I found that quoting and reading scripture helps to put it all in perspective, no matter what you're going through. Otherwise, when you're having a tough time, it can be hard to pray. Your prayers pretty much consist of saying, "Lord, help me," and you groan and moan through that. There's nothing wrong with that, but you end those prayer sessions pretty much how you started: focused on you and with little perspective.

YIELD

What do your prayers look like? Do they mostly consist of a list of things you want from God, or do they include praise, thanks, or even times of worship? Have you ever prayed scripture before? How might doing that change your prayer life?

WHEN BAD THINGS HAPPEN TO GOOD PEOPLE

One question I've certainly given some thought to since that period of my life is why God lets us go through those times to begin with. I wish I could say I've come up with some amazing answers that make it all worthwhile, but it's a mystery. Despite not having it all figured out, though, I do firmly believe that God uses it for good, and I did learn a few things during my days in the desert. Also, I think you come out being a much stronger person than before. I know I emerged with a stronger faith.

My time in the desert seemed to serve as a sort of refiner's fire. It kind of tests you to see what you're made of. For me, it gave me an amazing confidence. I had survived! It was affirming to know I had made it through and that I could do that again if I had to. I don't want to, but I could. So I know for sure that those times of testing strengthen your faith.

One other truth I came to grips with during my desert experience is that I am not in control. Even more alarming, I never will be. That can be a hard lesson for anyone to learn. It's easy to imagine that if we do all the "right" things, if we show up every week for Sunday school, if we eat plenty of fruits and vegetables, if we come in before curfew, if we love God and love our neighbors, we'll get a certain result. But life isn't like one of those experiments in chemistry class where if you add solution A to solution B, you'll know with certainty that you'll get reaction C. It's unpredictable. Sometimes you mix all the right ingredients together and what it produces is a great big mess. Not that you shouldn't continue to do the right things, just do them knowing that you won't get a guarantee of a nice, comfortable life in exchange for your obedience.

Any sense of control we have in this life really is an illusion. Job's story definitely teaches us that. And it seems like the more control you think you have, the more God works on teaching you to depend on Him for everything. I feel like I've done almost

YIELD

Do you think that ultimately you're in control of your life? What are you afraid would happen if you surrendered control? Have there been specific situations that have proven to you that you're really not in control? How did that make you feel when you realized it?

everything. I've won lots of awards, and my career success has brought me money, so I have the freedom to do things that aren't available to everyone. But having so much has taught me an important lesson. None of it is going to make me truly happy. I try to think of something new I can do, somewhere I can go, or something I can buy that will float my boat, and nothing does. I can't think of anything that I want to do that will really make me fulfilled. That's because only God can really, truly satisfy me. Job knew that. He wasn't happy because of all the things God gave Him. He was content when He rested in God's love. Having more opportunities let me learn that lesson a little earlier.

No matter how much we have (or don't have), we all have a choice. I know who I am and where I came from. I know God guides my every step and knows every hair on my head. I know He knows when I'm going to die and how long I'm going to live. It's my choice to surrender that control and to look at the big picture.

Job did, and he was eventually rewarded. I did, and I came out the other side a wiser, stronger person with a faith that's unshakeable. No, I don't have it all together. I still look up to others in my life, guys who lead by example. But I've got the important stuff down cold. I know I'm nothing without the Lord in my life. I know I'm not God, and I'm not in charge.

We're never going to fully understand the mysteries of God this side of heaven. Fortunately, we don't have to in order to love and serve Him. And as we do that, the road won't always be smooth. There will be mountaintop experiences, and, whether we like it or not, there will be valleys. We can't avoid them, but we can learn from them. So when you hit a rough patch, trust that you're there for a reason. And know that God will be there to see you through.

I've had many wonderful moments in my life, true high points that had me soaring. There have also been lows, disappointments, hurts, and losses that I still to this day don't understand. The one thing that was constant during all of these times was my faith in God. I knew that He didn't love me more when things were good and less when things were bad. Instead, He was simply there to love me through whatever was going on in my life.

Does how you feel about God change based on your circumstances? Are you more enthusiastic about your faith when things are going your way? Do you only turn to Him when you're in deep trouble and nothing else has worked? Imagine how you would feel if you had a friend who treated you the way you treat God.

Job proved he certainly wasn't a fair-weather friend to God. Through it all, he remained faithful. What did you think of as you read his story? What can you learn from it?

___

___

___

___

___

___

___

___

___

___

___

chapter eleven

Above All

First place. It's what athletes go to sleep dreaming about. It's the best you can hope for, the highest pinnacle, the top of the heap. Whether you're a spelling bee champ, a 4-H winner, or a high school track star, that blue ribbon means the same thing: you're the best in that field on that given day. If you've ever come in first in anything, you know it's an incredible feeling. There isn't much that matches it. You feel special, singled out, important.

First place finishes aren't that rare, though. We award blue ribbons in our own lives every day: "Best Friend," "Most Valuable Possession," "1st Place in My Heart." We may not actually hand them out, but we make decisions each day about what we're going to allow to become or remain most important to us. Some of those decisions are made by default or inaction on our part, others we consciously decide by what we do. But no matter how they're determined, the results are the same and the standings are recorded.

YIELD

What's ranking high in your life right now and where is God in the standings? Is He running a close second to your boyfriend or girlfriend? Is He slipping back in the pack lately, falling back to seventh or eighth place even, depending on what else you have going on that day and what else sparks your interest?

The problem is, God wants first place in your heart. Every day, He wants you to award Him that blue ribbon that says He and He alone is the most important thing in your life. Are you surprised by that? Do you wonder why the God of the universe cares how He finishes in the daily race to be first in your heart? It might also surprise you to find out that God is jealous over you.

Jealousy isn't usually a very pretty emotion and certainly not one we associate with God, but you only have to look at the beginning of the Ten Commandments to see that He isn't just asking politely, He demands first place in your life. In Exodus 20:2–3, He says, "I am the LORD your God. . . . You shall have no other gods before me." But that's not all. He goes on to add in verse 5, "For I, the LORD your God, am a jealous God."

Unlike when we're jealous, though, watching out for our own

best interests and what we want or what we think will make us happy at the moment, God isn't thinking of Himself alone. He has *our* best interests in mind. He wants to be first in our lives because He loves us and He wants what's best for us. God knows that when we're putting Him first, we're going to get His best in our lives. And there's nothing better than that.

If that's the case, why *wouldn't* we want to put God first in our lives? After all, we know He loved us enough to send His Son to die for our sins. Is there anybody else, any of the other people or things competing for first place in your life that can say they love you that much? I didn't think so.

YIELD

What keeps you from putting God first in your life? Are you afraid His best and your best won't be the same? Are you afraid your life won't turn out the way you planned or you won't get something you really want?

The song "Above All" is a great reminder of that for me. Unlike most of what I record, I didn't have anything to do with writing this song. It appears on my first worship project, simply titled *Worship*, and for that CD I was really concerned with trying to find ten to fifteen great worship songs. This was the first record where I didn't write every song on my album.

It's interesting because I have so many people who say, "I love your song!" and I tell them, "I didn't write 'Above All.'" I must have said that a thousand times. But I love it because it gives me a great opportunity to talk about Paul Baloche and Lenny LeBlanc, the two talented worship leaders and songwriters who *are* responsible for writing the song. You've probably sung Paul's song "Open the Eyes of My Heart" many times before in church or during a worship service, or you may have come across it on your local Christian radio station. In addition to his songwriting, Lenny has lent his musical talents to legendary artists like Roy Orbison, The Supremes, and Amy Grant, among others.

I first stumbled upon "Above All" while going through worship compilation CDs to find music for New River Fellowship in Franklin, Tennessee. I immediately knew it was a great song. It's so visual and a wonderful marriage of music and words. It made such an impact on me, in fact, that to this day I cry sometimes when I start to sing it. That's nothing compared to the first time I played it, though. I'll never forget that. It was at New River, and I lost it. I cried through the entire song. There is something about it that is very, very powerful. I can't explain it.

I guess that's why I decided I had to play it at the Inaugural Prayer Service at the Washington Cathedral when George W. Bush was sworn in as our 43rd president. I had only first heard it the month before, and it wasn't the song I was originally going to sing for the incoming president. It was going to be a very traditional service, and those who were doing the planning seemed to have their minds set on me doing a hymn. They even went so far as to suggest several songs the president liked. But once I found "Above All," I knew it was perfect. I thought, *That's what I've got to sing!*

There were consequences, though, of performing a song that was so new to me. If you go back and watch the footage it's funny because you can see that I've got little cheat sheets, tiny pieces of paper on the piano, to keep me from forgetting the words or music. Still, it was more than worth it to me.

Although the song was new to me, it had been written about three years earlier. I just hadn't heard it before. But once I made the discovery, I was going to make the most of it. It was a no-brainer to include it on *Worship* because I saw how it affected people everywhere when I sang it. I knew it had to be part of the lineup of that disc. Making it even more special, I'd met the songwriters on a worship tour I did with worship artist Don Moen. That connecting point was great because it meant I got to hear a few details about how the song came about. I'm still not sure exactly what inspired it, but Paul told me that as they were writing it together, these two grown men just kept crying. I was glad to hear I wasn't the only one. Apparently, it's really emotional for a lot of people.

YIELD

Has a song ever moved you that deeply? Has a time of worship ever brought about that kind of response? When you think about what God has done for you and how He still pursues you and wants to be part of your life, how does that make you feel?

AFTER YOU. NO, AFTER YOU!

There are many ways we can put God first in our lives. Often, it's as simple as including Him in our day. Do you segregate God, making Him a "church only" savior? He doesn't just hang around, waiting for you to take Him to youth group on Wednesday night or invite Him along to Sunday school. God wants to be part of everything you do.

Going to the mall? Take Him along and let Him influence your behavior and decisions. Is the way you're treating the salespeople, those you're shopping with, or the employees at the food court honoring to Him? Next, you might take Him along to basketball practice or to the gym. Does the way you respond to others on the court or in the weight room change when you make a conscious decision to put God first? Now imagine it's dinnertime, and as you sit down with your family, Jesus joins you as well. Do you react differently to your parents? Your brothers and sisters? Are you more patient? Now it's homework time. With God joining you as you study, does it change the effort you make? Will it affect whether or not you agree to share the answers with that guy who sits next to you in fourth period who didn't do the work? Finally, you're talking on the phone with a friend later that night. The conversation turns to a girl you don't really like. How is the conversation different when you invite God to listen in and when you don't?

Are you getting the idea? It takes effort to really give God first place in your life, but the benefits are huge. No one else you can award that ribbon to has the power to make as much of an impact.

YIELD

What parts of your day do you usually include God in? What parts of your day does He get excluded from? Why is that? What would happen if you really let God into every area of your life? How would your behavior change?

A TWO-WAY STREET

The really crazy part of this whole thing is that God doesn't just want to be first in our lives, He puts us first, too. Now if you really think about it, it makes perfect sense that the Creator of heaven and earth would want to take His rightful place in our lives. But what did we do in this particular case to deserve first place? What could we do that would be enough to deserve such a prize?

Absolutely nothing.

That's both sobering and a huge relief. There's nothing we *can* do to earn God's love. At the same time, there's nothing we *have to* do to earn God's love. He just gives it freely. That may not mean much until you look at the way we love each other. Often, even under the best of circumstances, our affection comes with strings attached. We give because we get. We love someone because it makes us feel good about ourselves or we get love in return. God, on the other hand, just loves us, knowing that in many cases the people He created aren't even going to love Him back. At the very least, it's certain we won't be able to love Him the way He deserves to be loved. And yet He carries on. He keeps loving us, keeps waiting patiently for us to get the message, to understand what's really important.

At the end of the day, there's one final truth we all need to grasp. It's what I try to communicate again and again when I lead worship. Sometimes we get so carried away living our lives, rushing to complete all the things we've deemed important, that it's easy for us to forget that it's not about us. It never was. While God loves us more than we can ask or imagine, He's the star of the show. He's the one who deserves all the attention, all the praise. Of course, He doesn't need us to tell Him that. Whatever place we choose to give Him in our lives, first place was awarded a long, long time ago, and He was the winner.

If the people and activities in your life were all in a race for first place, where would each rank in the standings today? How do those standings change based on how plugged in you are at church or how often you spend time reading your Bible or praying? How does what's important to you change based on who your friends are or who you're spending time with? Now is a wonderful time to get your priorities in line.

Rank what was important to you two years ago, five years ago, even ten years ago. Don't worry if you were in diapers then. You still had priorities. Naps, blankets, pacifiers, and parents are just a few of the things you probably counted as "most important" during your preschool years.

Now compare the standings and see how they've changed over time. Have things you once thought you'd die without lost importance over the years? What has taken their place? Now look at your current list. What items that currently rank near the top will still matter to you five years from now? And in ten years?

____

____

____

____

____

____

____

____

____

chapter Twelve

Raging Sea

Despite everything we've talked about, all the ways to ensure that you stay on track, survive having your faith tested, and remain plugged in, the Christian life can be hard. You can get tired. It can seem lonely. You might begin to feel like everyone else is having a great time while you're sitting home on Friday night with your principles. I wish I could tell you that wasn't the case, that if you believe hard enough and love God well enough, you'll never be sad or hurt or have anything bad happen to you.

Unfortunately, life doesn't work that way. Sometimes, despite having God on our side, the road seems really long, and it gets tempting to turn back. You might even find yourself wondering, *Why do I even bother?*

If that's true, I wrote the song "Raging Sea" just for you. I was in the studio with the band in northern California, and I wasn't planning to write anything else that day. In fact, I think we were actually in the middle of listening to a recording of "Signs" in the studio. Everyone was in a great mood, and it was definitely an "up" time. But from time to time, my head will go from one world to another. You wouldn't know it to look at me, but I'm gone. All of the sudden I've slipped out of the room, and I'm at the piano writing a new song.

So if I wasn't down or dealing with anything particularly dark in my own life or with those around me, why would I write a song like "Raging Sea" that deals with hard times? I'm honestly convinced it was the voices of others that inspired me on that day. I hear a lot of people's painful stories. I get e-mail messages from some on my Web site, and others line up after shows to tell me what they're going through. Most of them are dealing with something in their life that has sent them reeling. I see them at church, too, people who just never seem to get a break in life, and it makes me wonder why.

I think I store a lot of that in my head, and I don't forget those people until, eventually, it just starts flooding out. I become compelled, and their story comes out through my fingers. Then all of a sudden, I'm writing something like "Raging Sea." It's amazing how you can be having a great time, and then before you know it, it happens. I honestly think God orchestrates those moments of creativity, and I never know when they're coming.

Despite the heavy subject matter, "Raging Sea" isn't a song without hope. Even when I'm listening to these painful stories, I'm confident there's a way out. God has told us it's true. Maybe that's why this song is written from God's perspective. I call it a "God-to-man" lyric. I'm not saying this is what God told me. It's not prophetic. It's just what I perceive as the heart of God. As a result, I think the song reaches down from heaven and pierces the heart of people who are hurting.

I know that happened in at least one case. There's a girl who I e-mail fairly regularly since meeting her several years ago after a big Christian music festival in New York. She's paralyzed and has been in a wheelchair for fourteen years following a car wreck. Her life is difficult, to say the least. She can barely talk, but she managed to e-mail me and say, "You have no idea. That song was written for me."

YIELD

Have there been circumstances in your own life that have left you asking God why? Did they cause you to doubt that God really cared? How did you get through those tough times?

BEEN THERE, DONE THAT

She's not the only one who needed to hear that message. Despite my own strong faith, there are times and events that tempt me to question, "What am I doing this for?" I have to admit there are days when I feel like I'm just not in touch with reality, and I start to go, "I'm a fraud. I'm not what people think I am." But then I revert back to the songs, and they remind me of what's true. It's funny how easy it is to forget, to get caught up in doubting and not remember all God has done in my life.

The challenges that tempt you to lose hope or find life losing its meaning are probably different in your life. Maybe you find yourself feeling hopeless because of the things that are missing in your life. It could be that you've never had a role model or a solid foundation. There isn't anyone to lead the way, and you're afraid you can't make it on your own. Or maybe it has to do with what's been done to you. Circumstances have you questioning how God can ever make anything good out of your life.

I'm here to tell you that God is bigger than all of that. I have seen it proven in the lives of those close to me. My mentor, Don, whom I consider to be one of the wisest and most godly men I know, was abused when he was younger. His life was in shambles. And my mom went through some difficult years as well. My real grandmother walked out on my mother and her three siblings when my mom was just six years old. Her dad eventually remarried a wonderful lady, so things turned around, but Mom had every reason to be bitter. So did Don. But they chose to turn toward God in their hurt instead of turning away. My mom determined that she was never going to do that to her own kids, while Don became a pastor and helped thousands of others who were hurting. They both decided to make the best of what they'd been given, and God blessed them.

Those aren't the only examples. I could list hundreds. Throughout the years, I've seen God at work in desperate situations. The trick is, you have to choose to believe when sometimes it seems there's absolutely no reason to believe. At those times, you have to get beyond feelings and have faith that what God says is true despite your circumstances. In Jeremiah 29:11, a wonderful promise is made: "'For I know the plans I have for you,' declares the LORD, 'plans to prosper you and not to harm you, plans to give you hope and a future.'"

Is that true or is that false? You have to make the decision to believe it. No one can do that for you. As for me, I believe it's true, and I think if you'll stand on that and believe that no matter what, then things are sure to turn around.

I know that's easier said than done, but just saying it is an exercise in obedience. Determining that you're going to believe even when the feelings aren't there is often the first step. Sometimes, just by saying it, you can move toward believing it. Does that mean that by uttering those few words everything wrong in your life will suddenly become right? Hardly. There's no magic prayer that will make your parents get back together, your friends turn to God, or your grades miraculously improve. But I do believe God will give you the strength to weather those storms and come out on the other side.

YIELD

How big of a part do feelings play in your faith? What does that mean when you encounter difficulties or disappointments? Is it harder to believe God is who He says He is or that He has your best interests in mind?

SEEING ISN'T ALWAYS BELIEVING

My own raging sea probably comes from caring about others too much. If I find myself feeling weary or like the road is too long, it's usually because I find myself trying to fix too many things, and I spread myself too thin. I care so much about other people's hurts that I get into a predicament. Before I know it, I'm trying to help everybody while also trying to be a good husband and father and hold down my job and do it well. Then all the sudden, in the middle of all these things, something bad happens to me or someone I love, and I'm swept away into a sea of doubt or despair.

During those times, it can be easy to lose sight of God. He promises that He will never leave us or forsake us, but when tough times come, He can seem awfully far away. This is a good time to remind ourselves that feelings aren't fact. To really grasp this, it might help to imagine you're a pilot. When bad weather hits, pilots don't use what they see or feel to fly the plane because storms can render their instincts unreliable. Instead, they use a series of high tech instruments to get them on the ground safely. God wants us to do the same. When tough times come (and they *will* come), instead of relying on how you feel or what your bruised and battered heart tells you, use what you know to be true to guide you back to solid ground. Trust what the Bible says and what you've learned as you've studied it, and your feelings won't override your faith.

In the end, it really does come down to believing. It's a mystery to me why God often feels so far away when we need Him most. I know He's there even though it doesn't feel like He is, but it's still hard to fathom. It just goes to show you that you can't base everything on emotions. The bottom line is you have to believe. After all, if you need proof, then it's not faith. It's something else.

For me, that means that even though I don't see Him, I know He's real. Sometimes I don't feel Him, but I still believe He's near. He said He would be, so I have faith that He's all around me, whatever my emotions are on that particular day. Not that it isn't great when you feel it. It's wonderful when you experience something that you know could have only come about through God, when you see miraculous things happen in your life or the lives of others. But that can't be all your faith is about. Otherwise, when your life takes a left turn and things are difficult and He doesn't feel near, where will that leave you?

YIELD

Why do you think God allows us to go through hard times? What do you learn during trials that you don't learn in your daily walk with Christ?

NO PAIN, NO GAIN

Any high school athlete has probably heard the saying: "No pain, no gain." I really do believe God allows certain things to happen for a reason. I have no idea why He allows some people to go through certain things, and I won't until I see Him face to face, but I do believe there is a reason for the suffering we endure here on this earth. I have lots of questions, but deep down I know His ways are higher than our ways. Maybe He allows some things to happen to strengthen our faith. At the time you're going through it, you're saying, "This is no fun, this is not going to strengthen my faith. I am not digging this part of my life." But it's at those times that He's really working in you.

Right now, that can be hard to believe, but one day we'll see the whole picture, and I'm convinced that we'll go, "Oh, I didn't think about that!" Suddenly, it will all be clear. Of course, to hold on until that day takes a tremendous amount of faith. So much of what we do and how we operate and conduct our lives consists of reminding ourselves that He's in control when it doesn't seem like He is.

Not everyone can accept that. For some, the crashing waves of life get to be too much for them, and they give up. I have friends who have come to that point, and it's really, really sad to see. Without getting too judgmental, I realize I could have easily been that person. So when I see someone go down or give up, it really makes me want to stand a little taller in my faith and say, "I'm not going to let that happen to me."

To make sure I'm protected, I start by stepping up the accountability because I think we're all susceptible to falling off the cliff. Every one of us. I don't care who you are, there's always that possibility it could happen, so you say, "I'm going to do whatever I have to do to make sure that it doesn't happen to me." That means you set parameters, and you determine boundaries and limits before you get into trouble, because if you start playing with fire, I can guarantee you're going to get burned.

As for those friends who got weary of trying and gave up the fight, my responsibility to them hasn't changed. I continue to love them. And I pray that God will come to their rescue and that they'll come to their senses and realize the fight's not over. As long as we're still breathing, there's hope.

It's so easy to believe in God when everything's going right in our lives. But our faith really becomes real when it's all we're holding on to. We may not feel like believing; we may wonder where God is in our hurting; we may even begin to think we made a mistake by following Him in the first place. But when we're at that place, God can do some amazing things—if only we'll let Him.

God doesn't need fair-weather friends. Those who show up for the games or fun of youth group or show a sudden interest in the Bible because that cute guy with a locker near theirs is a Christian will have a hard time standing firm when times get tough. That's why we need to prepare ahead of time. You wouldn't head out into a storm without a raincoat or other provisions. In the same way, you can plan for the storms of life.

Reading your Bible, memorizing scripture, attending Bible study and church, choosing friends who hold you accountable—all of these are great ways to ensure you'll be ready when the waves come crashing in. Not that you won't get knocked down occasionally (we all do), but these spiritual exercises will help you have the strength needed to weather whatever comes your way.

What are some exercises you can do today to build your spiritual strength? How are you helping others to build theirs? How can these things improve your daily walk with God?

For more information about the organizations Michael mentions, check out:

Compassion International™
Colorado Springs, CO 80997
Phone: 800-336-7676
www.compassion.com

Kanakuk Kamps
1353 Lakeshore Drive
Branson, MO 65616-9470
Phone: 417-266-3000
Fax: 417-239-3200
www.kanakuk.com

Kids Across America
1429 Lakeshore Drive
Branson, MO 65616
Phone: 417-266-4000
Fax: 417-266-4001
www.kidsacrossamerica.org

Rocketown
401 Sixth Avenue South
Nashville, TN 37203
Event Hotline: 615-843-4000
General Office: 615-843-4001
www.rocketown.org